The Memoirs of Kenneth Loren Chard

The Memoirs of Kenneth Loren Chard

By Kenneth L. Chard

Edited & Introduction by Thea Chard

The Memoirs of Kenneth Loren Chard

Copyright © 2015 by Kenneth L. Chard

ALL RIGHTS RESERVED

All photographs are courtesy of the author's family, except on page 40 where indicated: reprinted with permission courtesy of Vetfriends.com, or as part of the Public Domain via Wikimedia Commons.

No part of this book may be reproduced in any written, electronic, recording, or photocopying without written permission of the publisher. The exception would be in the case of brief quotations embodied in the critical articles or reviews and pages where permission is specifically granted by the publisher or author.

Although every precaution has been taken to verify the accuracy of the information contained herein, the author and publisher assume no responsibility for any errors or omissions. No liability is assumed for damages that may result from the use of information contained within.

Printed & Bound in the United States of America

First Edition, First Printing: October 2015

Cover design by Thea Chard
Book design by Thea Chard
Edited by Thea Chard

Published by Rainy City Press

Hardcover: ISBN 978-0-9968993-0-7
Paperback: ISBN 978-0-9968993-2-1
eBook: ISBN 978-0-9968993-1-4

For Ken.

Table of Contents

Introduction	**8**
Chard Family History	**14**
Beginnings	**15**
Oregon Bound	**20**
Foundations	**27**
Homesteading	**30**
The War Years	**36**
Home Again	**57**
Family Life	**64**
New Beginnings	**67**
Q&A with Ken	**70**
About the Author	**75**

INTRODUCTION

NARROWING DOWN THE many memories I have of my grandfather to a precious few fit to illustrate a life is, to say the least, impossible, especially when that life is one that turned out to be quite extraordinary in some of the least typical ways. But it's those small, seemingly insignificant things about Ken—the little quirks and stories—that I will remember and cherish most about him.

I will remember the way he always wore cowboy boots, at least as long as he could pull those suckers on, no matter the day. He had at least one pair, but more often several, fit for every occasion. They became an extension of his person and his persona. They were, quite literally, the shoes he chose to walk the world in for the majority of his life.

I will always remember how he would wake up at the crack of dawn and start cooking breakfast for everyone in the house, the heels of his boots click-clacking on the floor as he cracked each egg and sizzled bacon, slice by slice. As a child, whenever we would come to visit, I would wake up to the sound of Grandpa tinkering around the kitchen and the sweet, salty smell of bacon cooking before the sun rose. I would jump out of bed and delight in breakfast preparations. Even as a little girl, I appreciated these few moments we shared, just grandfather and granddaughter, every morning, before the rest of the house awoke and joined in our early risers' routine. Now, thinking back, I wonder if I don't have Ken to blame for my lifelong love affair with bacon. It all began there, in that kitchen.

I remember one morning—I was probably no more than five years old—I woke up in the same way, scurrying from my bed in the living room to the kitchen, where I would climb up on one of the kitchen stools and plop down, legs dangling, while he cooked. I pretended I was overseeing the operation, ensuring that every piece was crisped to perfection. Grandpa was standing there, already dressed for the day, a pair of his good boots on, skillet in hand, transferring each piece one by one to a plate where a bed of paper towels would soak up the grease. After a few slices, he'd lay another towel down and begin again, layering the strips of bacon, crisscrossed, like the logs in the Lincoln Logs game he and Sharon saved for us grandkids to play with on visits.

Every time he turned his back to face the skillet, I would surreptitiously slide a strip off the plate and chomp away in secret glee. This went on for several minutes, my sneaky grease-covered fingers unnoticed, until an entire pound of bacon meant to feed five was gone. The rest of the house awoke to the sound of Ken hollering after me as I ran to hide, not even fully realizing myself what I'd done. But the next day we were back to the same old routine. Bacon never tasted quite as good as when Grandpa Ken made it.

I will always remember how on those visits, Grandpa would keep me up late to teach me some new card game, or another with dice, one which usually involved shouting out "bullshit!" to call someone's bluff, and the way he would amend this to "bull-hickey!" or something else equally as funny in all its age-appropriate-ness.

I will always remember how Ken and Sharon's home always felt in the holiday spirit, no matter the time of year, and how from Thanksgiving to New Year's the living room would transform into a mini Christmas Village and every year Ken would add a new piece—a structure, a chapel, a town square, a train winding its way through the growing community.

I will always remember how, after those early morning breakfasts, Grandpa would pack up and go for a round of early morning golf, and how he and my dad would sneak me onto the course with them and wait until we were far enough away from the office to let me swing a few, those rebels. He got more done before 9 a.m. than most people did all day.

I will always remember the way he pronounced Washington "War-shing-ton," and Italian "I-talian," and no matter how many times you reminded him that it wasn't pronounced "I-taly," he was never swayed, and how it was better that way.

And I will always remember the way he told stories—his candor and the rhythm of his speech; the way he would accentuate critical plot points with "gosh" and "gee-golly!" and a slap on the knee.

He always had the most fascinating stories, full of grit and nostalgia, of a different kind of life—before electricity and indoor plumbing, cell phones and winters weathered safely indoors. There were so many of these stories and he derived so much joy out of telling them, something I only truly came to fully appreciate near the end, after Ken wrote out his entire life story on 130 handwritten pages and mailed the only copy to me to turn into this book, the story of his life.

Ken sent me his memoirs a few months before he passed. Written in scrawling pencil, all of it was composed in cursive, much of it in shorthand, the rest of it in sprawling, almost stream-of-consciousness sentences, some of which either didn't end, or sat truncated and unfinished. Some thoughts were so clear—crystal memories married to the page in squiggly script—others were half-thoughts; incomplete sentences, bits of intention here, little gems of recollection there.

The manuscript was riddled with misspellings, something Ken joked about throughout the pages himself and often to me. But this made it more rich, somehow: an undeniably potent, raw artifact right out of his own history. He wrote the words as he would have spoken them out loud, to all of us, as if he were telling us one of his wonderful stories, but this story was the story; the whole thing, as he wanted it told. Singapore became "Sing a poor"; Saipan became "Sapen"; boatswain became "boatson"; hustle and bustle became "husell and busell"; Bikini became "Bekinies" (he was talking about the string of islands in the Pacific Ocean, not the article of clothing, don't worry). Grandpa became "grandpaw," but for some reason, only half the time. Some words became interchangeable—"of" and "off"; "then" and "than"; "will" and "well"—while others took five or six attempted readings before they revealed themselves within the context of the page.

It took me over a year chipping away on nights and weekends to finish transcribing the thing. I thought of stopping there, printing it out and distributing it—and maybe I should have—but I couldn't bring myself to conclude it just yet; it all felt so unfinished. Ken's thoughts were there, word for word, but the resulting text was incomplete somehow—fragmented, at a few points incoherent, sentences stagnated, facts jumbled, a few threads in the story left loose and hanging. I set about editing; researching places and events mentioned in the text, tying together gaps in the timeline, corroborating historical facts, and doing my best to smooth over the few places where Ken's words and his thoughts appeared to diverge.

It was important to me that Ken's words were not changed and his thoughts were left unaltered—if a sentence was written without a conjunction, though the meaning itself was easily understood, it was left that way. If and only when a sentence was unreadable without the addition of a certain missing word, would that piece, as best as I could interpret it, be added in brackets (looking something [like] this). When Ken referenced historical events—especially throughout his childhood and during his recollections from World War II—I added footnotes where I thought it might clarify a fact, or add information of relevance or of interest, for those who may want to do further reading.

Throughout this process I came across a number of historical images from the time that add color and context to the picture Ken so vividly painted for us. Because so few photographs from that time are available (though many from the family were given and reprinted in these pages), I included as many historical images as I could secure the rights to print. One such image was a photo of the USS YMS 65, the minesweeper Ken was stationed on during the war, taken in 1943. The only reliable image I could find of this ship was on a website dedicated to reuniting veterans of the United States Armed Forces, called VetFriends.com. After sharing Ken's story with them along with the plans to posthumously publish his memoir, the organization very graciously granted permission for this photo to be reprinted here, alongside Ken's memories of his time aboard. Being able to actually see the vessel as Ken recounts it can only be described as a visceral experience.

You'll find that proper grammar and punctuation rules were, on the whole, disregarded—laissez faire in their application, added more for effect and pacing than adherence to any actual publishing standards. Proper nouns were anointed generously—the Doctor, the Pharmacist, the Bank—all given a place of power and respect in Ken's mind through the mere inclusion of a single capital letter.

As you read Ken's memories from his life, I hope you'll hear his voice, his excited candor and intonation; the unique way he pronounced certain things and emphasized others, just as if he were speaking directly to you. In a way, that's exactly what this book has done—given him a way to continue to tell us, his loved ones, all of the stories from his past far into the beyond.

I have never been so honored as when Ken asked me to take his words and turn them into a book that he could share with his family and leave with us to love and remember him by after he'd gone. I'm only sorry that he never got to see the finished copy and hold it in his hands, feeling pride in the new tangibility of the life he lived and in sharing it with all of us.

For the long wait, I apologize. I hope the experience of reading Ken's memoirs will be as rewarding for you as the task of putting this book together has been for me.

The reading of these pages will be, no doubt, an inherently personal experience for each of us. For me, it brought new insight into the grandfather I knew and the many men he was before then—always a part of him, though never seen directly through my own eyes.

To Ken I say, thank you for passing on your stories to us—your nature, your do-it-yourself attitude, your gusto and fervor, are all things I see in my dad, who in turn passed them to me. When I see his face, I see your face. When I hear him say "War-shing-ton" I hear your voice repeat it over and over like a whisper in my head, and I smile every time.

In a way it's fitting that Ken said goodbye to us in the winter, a time when family gets together to share meals and memories and love. While winter is not upon us yet, it's fast approaching, and with it will come all the memories of Ken, still fresh in our minds and our hearts. I'm lucky in that I get to carry Ken with me every winter, when I wrap myself up in his old navy peacoat, another artifact from his life and the war that was passed on to my dad, who in turn passed it on to me. I have spent many cold months warm in Ken's coat, holding his memory in my heart, hearing his voice stream through my head and my fingers, as I finished the last thing he ever asked me to do—sharing his life's story with his family as a final goodbye. Now that it's done, I see that it isn't actually a goodbye at all. It's a new beginning.

Through this book, we all get to carry a bit of Ken with us, and though it's been nearly three years since his passing, his words don't read as a goodbye letter; they spring off the page, take on his voice, and unfold like a good conversation, the ones we all so remember sharing with him. As I finished writing this, I heard Ken's chuckle—that little laugh, almost a grunt, filled with satisfaction and closeness and love—and I feel more than ever that he is still with us, today and every day, in these memories put to page and these stories he always told, now left to us to tell on.

—Thea Chard
September 2015

Chard Family History

I'VE BEEN ASKED to write down what I had done and remembered in my life. I will start this with some background.

My father, Ewen Cyrus Chard, was born in 1896 from a family of seven children: five boys, two girls. He was the oldest boy. He only attended school through fourth grade, as he had to work on the farm. He was drafted into the army in 1919 and served as a medic. He did not go overseas. His service time was at Chicago and while there it was wintertime when the flu hit. Many soldiers died and they stacked them outside like cordwood.

He was discharged and returned home at Lucas, Kansas. He then met my mom, Jessie Ann Metland, born in 1898. She was from a family of seven children: five girls and two boys. Mom did make it through high school. Her and dad met and were married and drove a matched team and covered wagon to Giltner, Nebraska, to work on a farm there.

Five of us kids were born there: Berl Dean, Betty Jean, Peggy May, Kenneth Loran and Patty Patricia. Berl Dean passed away when he was three years old.[1]

We moved back to Lucas, Kansas and Dad took over the Chard farms and Jackie Gerald Chard was born.

---

1 Berl Dean passed after contracting bronchitis, according to Ken.

Beginnings

I'll start this back in Lucas, Kansas. What year I am not sure, but one day we were just coming to the house in the truck and I was standing on the ground and holding onto the door of the truck and lightning struck a large cottonwood tree 20 to 30 feet from the truck, and as I was on the ground by the truck, I was unconscious for a short while. Others in the truck were all OK. The tree was split and was tore into small pieces. Tree was 100 feet tall.

Remembering in summertime when the mulberry tree's fruit would get ripe we would spread blankets under the tree and then shake the tree limbs and the ripe berries would fall and we would eat these with sugar and cream. Later in my life I went back to Kansas and these berries tasted terrible.

I started school at a small school called Fox Creek School. There were seven kids in school—Betty, Peggy, myself, Lily Brown, Jr., Kenneth Bunker and Bella Milkem. First grade through eighth grade. Same teacher.

We walked to school about a mile and a half. One day on our way home we had to pass Jasper and Nettie Brown's place and Nettie was unstable and she came out yelling at us with a knife. We took off running and when she got pretty close the girls would go under a fence and drag me. When Nettie would get through the fence we would go back through the fence and she finally gave up. Boy we were scared. Folks had a talk with Jasper. I just knew that knife was two feet long, but probably only a small butcher knife.

Dust storms were prevalent along with drought. Dad was with

Uncle Jack going down to Texas buying feed for the cattle. As the pastures were dried up, crops were dying in the fields. A lot of the dust was reddish in color and the dust would drift and cattle would get out as the drifts would be higher then fences.

Mom and Dad put wet sheets over windows to help keep dust out of the house. When they set the table for meals, the plates, bowls, etc. were upside down and when we were ready to eat, we would turn our plate over and there would be a clean spot where the plate was.

Mom and I planted a garden up by the windmill as we could water and have a good crop. Dust storms was still blowing, but we finally had a wet spring and crops looked real good. Corn was five to six feet high, wheat was heading out.

And then the grasshoppers came and the sky turned dark and it sounded like airplanes. They came in the mid-afternoon and by the next morning corn and wheat was completely gone, eaten to the ground. All the leaves on the trees was eaten; they ate the paint from the house and barn; they even ate the softer grain in shovels and fork wooden handles. And needless to say our garden was gone, eaten to the ground.

And just prior to this time, during the dust storms, one afternoon a large black dust cloud hung over 40 to 50 feet, and then five large cone-type funnels started in the dust cloud. Needless to say we spent another night in the cellar.

Times were tough, but we always set at the table as a family for all three meals together and it was a happy time at our table no matter how little there was to eat. And many times there wasn't much on the table.

Being farmers we had chickens, pigs, cows, so we had eggs, chicken and meat. Pigs were used for all types of pork, such as bacon, sausage, pork chops, ribs, ham and shoulders. There was very little of a pig that wasn't used or eaten.

Mom and dad smoked most of the pork meat. After smoking,

they would wrap meat with newsprint and dip in white wash and let dry and do it a second time and the meat inside stayed good up to a year. Milk from cows of which we separated so as to have cream to churn for butter, and the skim milk was used to soak barley for pig feed.

In the early 30s not only the Great Depression, but the drought made it very difficult to make a living.

We had a Collie dog who disliked snakes and one afternoon we heard him barking and barking, growling, so we went to check and in the pasture he had two large bull snakes. Each snake were six to seven feet long and they were mad and would strike at the dog, who kept them together as he circled them. Us kids went told mom and she got her hoe, as dad kept it sharp, and she didn't like bull snakes as they would go in the chicken house and suck up the eggs. It took about a minute; both snakes had no heads.

Along this same time we went to gather eggs one evening and a bull snake was in one nest and swallowed a hole egg, crawled through a knothole to the next nest and again swallowed another egg, and at this time the snake was stuck and since he couldn't back up or go forward because the eggs were too large to pass through the knothole. So again Mom showed up with her hoe and one more snake was cut into right between the eggs and both were salvaged.

We had quite a few milk cows and one of the cows was about to have a new little calf. I would run out every little bit checking on her as I was wondering what kind of calf it would be. And sure enough she had her calf and I wanted to pet it, however cow was not pleased of me. Getting close to her newborn as she snorted at me and moved towards me, and I let out running toward the gate. I was afraid she was going to knock me down so I kept on looking back to see if she was getting closer. In Kansas we had stone posts for the fences.

These posts were about 10 inches square and eight feet long. While I was looking back to check on cow I ran into the stone post. The old cow was brushing and licking blood from my face by the time the folks got there. Funny, after that I could pet and play with the calf and the cow didn't mind at all. I still wear that scar's yet to this day.

Mom called Dad, 'Poppy'.

Until he ignored Mom, she would say, "Ewen, we are moving to Oregon."

So some very hectic days follow his farm sale. They had heard and had received information on land in Oregon—new land being opened up under the Owyhee Dam Project—and they knew Archie and Vivian Smith already had moved out there and had bought a small acreage.

They were making all kinds of discussions such as how were they going to get the household goods, equipment, tractor, etc. to Oregon. Dad went to an auto repair shop and rebuilt the 1927 Chevy four-door car. This was fall of 1935. Dad loaded the cattle, five cows and equipment and household in a railroad car and shipped it to Nyssa, Oregon. Dad rode in the car with the cattle, which needed to be milked both morning and night, and he gave the milk to the train men and bums along sidings, etc.

One of my favorite days was butchering day. Actually, it took several days to complete. Dad always made sure the pigs would be a least 200 pounds or heavier.

When this day came a three-leg, 10-foot-high lift was made with a double pulley rope stretcher to hang the pigs over the hot water.

First pigs were killed by shooting them in the head, then cutting their throats to bleed them out. The pig would then be lifted by the three-leg lift and dipped into the hot water. When he was lifted out they had scrapers to remove the hair, than placed the pig on a large table where they cut him up, like hams, shoulders, pork chops, bacon, etc. All of the fat was heated and made lard. Sometimes the pigs were turned the wrong side out, scrubbed and scraped clean for making sausage links. Dad and Mom always butchered eight hogs, one for each member of the family and one for company.

All of this meat was put into smoke house and cured by the heat of smoke. When this was completed the hams—all of the cured and smoked meat—was wrapped in newsprint and dipped in white wash paint and left hanging in the smoke house. Meat would stay good this way for about a year. When broken open you had to use it and I think Mom and Dad pretty well used everything on a pig except the squeal.

Oh yes, a lot of the fat was heated, put in a press and made a liquid fat, which Mom would make lye soap with filtered ashes and liquid fat lye.

I really liked the smoke house to play in. We did not ever have a smoke house in Oregon. So that left Mom and five kids to drive to Oregon. Uncle Charlie Metland, Mom's youngest brother, came and drove the 1927 Chevy to Oregon. Wyatt and June Smith came with us in a 1933 Pontiac.

Oregon Bound

The trip to Oregon for me at nine years old seemed like a long dream and we would not ever get to Oregon. I should say there was many signs at various places saying "detour" and I kept on wondering when we would get to Detour and why was there so many towns named this in every state, and finally Mom got it across to me detour meant a change in the route or highway we were traveling.

We stayed in little cabins on our way. Most cabins had a bed, a small counter and wash pan, and cold water, and most of them had a small wood or coal stove. Outdoor outhouses.

I remember somewhere in Wyoming we had stopped for the night and I went on a hillside and was playing on a rocky hillside and fell down and a large rock came down on my back left foot and of course it wasn't just bruised, it had bone broke, so Uncle Charlie held me down and Mom put the bone back in place, and needless to say it hurt for some time. But Mom kept it wrapped and it healed after we made it to Oregon.

Just before we arrived the 1927 Chevy had a vacuum pump for gasoline to the engine instead of a fuel pump. So whenever you started up a hill your engine did not produce enough vacuum to draw gasoline from the tank to the engine, therefore the vacuum tank held about one-half gallon and when it was out the engine died. We would then turn around and let gravity fill the vacuum and continue backing up the hill, so to get to Oregon we drove forwards and backwards—I would say 90 percent forwards and 10 percent backwards.

We landed in Nyssa, Oregon in October 1935. The folks put up a two-room tent on Archie Smith's place. By this time winter had set in and the folks were real close to being broke. But Dad, Wyatt and Uncle Charlie got a job taking out old apple orchards. They could have the apples on the trees before pulling them up and sawing up the wood into stove links, and they received half the wood.

It was a very cold winter. We had to walk two and a half miles to school and back. The folks had enough money to buy flour and corn meal.

The winter of 1935 and 1936, when we were in the tent, all of us kids came down with Scarlet fever. Both Peggy and Jack ended up with enlarged hearts. We didn't have any sugar, so Mom made pancakes and we had butter from the cows and Mom made apple butter. We had that on biscuits for lunches, as that was the only sweets we had.

We made it through winter and Dad started looking for land. The CCC[1] boys had pretty well finished irrigation ditches. And about this time Dad received his World War One Kansas bonus check. So Dad bought 40 acres just above Archie Smith's place. I am not sure what the land was being sold for, but heard later on about four to five dollars an acre. Dad also loaned two brothers money for down payments on their places. Each had 40 acres.

I should inject at this time there were jackrabbits—not just a few, but millions. In fact, I killed many with my beanie flipper and small rocks. When you walked through the sage brush a grey mass of rabbits would move. The CCC boys cut up carrots and poisoned them. They threw these out all over the area and wiped out the rabbits.

I believe winter of 1936 was coming soon and we moved from the Smith's to our farm. Again it was the two tents they called sheep tents. They had a wood frame and wood floors and two-foot high sides made of one inch by 12 inch by three-quarter inch wood, and wood rafters every four feet or so for the tent to go over. The big tent held the old-fashioned cook stove, table, chairs, and also a cabinet type that had tip out flour, sugar, doors. Also we had some orange crates standing on end for various kitchen items. I think Mom had a

---

1 Civilian Conservation Corps (CCC) was a United States public works relief program, one of the first programs of President Franklin D. Roosevelt's New Deal, which provided jobs in natural resource conservation to over three million young men during the near decade it operated, from 1933 to 1942. More information here: www.ccclegacy.org.

rocking chair. This room was 12 by 14 feet square with two doors, one from the outside and the other into the bedroom tent, approximately 10 feet by 12 feet. We had three beds: Mom and Dad's, the three girls' bed, and my brother and I had the other one. Clothes were hung from the ridgepole down the center of the tent. Boxes under beds held underclothes, etc.

One thing you learn real quick as it's cold outside and warmer inside is don't touch the tent above you because it will start dripping and by morning you would be wet. Bed would be wet, all of which then had to be taken outside and hung on the clothesline to dry.

The only heat we had was the old cook stove and that was one of my jobs, to cut sagebrush and cut into stove links. We had a double-blade axe Dad had bought, two work horses, and I would use them and cut a wagon load of sagebrush each night. Also when we got home from school my sisters Betty, Peggy and Patty, we would all have two, two gallon water cans, and Patty had two one-half gallon buckets and we would walk to Archie Smith's and fill buckets with water and walk back. It was about one mile round trip. I had to fill five boxes of sagebrush, then help milk the cows and I believe we were milking eight heads at that time. When cows were milked we had a hand-cranked separator so we had cream to churn butter. The skim milk was mixed with barley and set soaked for 12 hours and then fed to the pigs. All of the cows had calves and they had to be fed as well as cows and horses. Dad and I build a temporary barn out of poles and chicken wire, made walls of straw two feet thick, used poles across the tops again wire, straw and dirt. All was fine until a windstorm came up and I was inside milking. Down come barn, cows were knocked down and one laying kicking on me. I was hollering as loud as I could. Dad came, started throwing poles away fence material, jerking cattle up and finally got to me. I wasn't hurt too bad, covered with cow doo doo. Just another day on the farm.

I should say the 40 acres was a square plot and the railroad ran across our land and was built to build the Owyhee Dam. They moved most of the metal by rail to the dam site. Dam was complete in 1935, backing up water for 75 miles and the water was to be used to irrigate the land below the dam.

Spring finally came; Dad was breaking workhorses by leveling some sand dunes on the lower end of our place. He would hook the two unbroke horses between our two and had them hooked to a fresno-type scraper. It had runners on the backside and you would fill scrapper with dirt and when you dumped it you went and done it time after time. He leveled the lower end by breaking workhorses.

He bought a steel-wheeled McKormick Dearing tractor from Kansas. When you hit soft, sandy soil this tractor couldn't pull anything, it would just shake and not move. So everything was done by horsepower. Mom was planting a king size garden. Also she planted several rows of tams sunflowers on west side of the tent for shade in the evening. The garden was mom and my job to irrigate, plant, weed, etc., and I must say mom said we will never go hungry as we did in Kansas. We planted sweet corn like five rows this week, five more next week, doing this three or four times—we had sweet corn most all summer. We had green beans, peas, carrots, onions, radishes (both red and white), lettuces (both leaf and head), cabbage, kohlrabi, egg plant, tomatoes of all type: plain, large, red, small, salad-type, yellow. You name it we grew it—peanuts, potatoes, sweet potatoes, horseradishes, cucumbers, muskmelon, watermelon, pumpkin—you name it, she grew it. Mom sent for a pressure cooker so she could can what we were growing.

She canned like 300 quarts green beans, 300 pinto peas, 500 quarts tomatoes, carrots, etc. She made sweet pickles, dill pickles, cabbage was made into sauerkraut. We would go over to Emmett, Idaho, where all types of fruit was grown. She canned like 500 half gallons of peaches, pears, 500 quarts of plums, cherries, apricots.

And to prepare all of this food, five kids helped to snap green beans, shell peas, and shell beans. Plus one heck a lot of wood to heat the pressure cooker.

Also Dad and I were digging a well. It was four feet square and 45 feet deep. We had lots of water in this well and water was hard, tasted real good and cold. Winter time Patty and my job was to pump water for horses and cattle. I will say no horse, cow, calf drink one drop until tank was full. I could throw a cloud and drive them away until tank was full. Dad said we had to fill tank before we could quit pumping.

Maybe we should say I was in the fourth grade when we came to Oregon and coming from a school of seven kids to a school at Oregon Trail with about 40 kids was too much so I spent the two years in the fourth grade. It was rather unsettling being a dumb kid and not passing. I never flunked out again.

It was tough times not only for us kids but Mom and Dad.

Fall came and again the garden work was to store everything we could—potatoes and sweet potatoes—in cellar. Onions hung in cellar to be dried. Watermelon, muskmelon, eggplant, was placed in straw stack and they lasted into late November.

Mom and Dad ground up the horseradish and put in pint jars. Talk about hot and mean. It was hot.

That fall the government opened a lot of land up to Homestead. They would give you 160 acres and you had three years to improve by putting in crops, building a house to live in and breaking up in the land and planting the crops. Many of these farms built basement houses and in future built their house on top of the basement.

Grandpa and grandma Metland from Nebraska homesteaded; Uncle Ernie and Aunt Lucella Smith; Uncle Russel and Aunt Jenny Talbot and their children, which totaled 22 people staying with us in the two-room tent. It was rather crowded but seemed everyone chipped in and they all found land and Homestead Act. Grandpa and Grandma built a three-room house, both uncles built basements and moved onto their land.

It was a very busy time for Dad and Mom. Dad had barley, oats as cover crop over alfalfa hay. Other words barley and oats, both of which were harvested, protected the alfalfa seedling to take over the land and be able to grow.

I will say my Dad was a very good farmer. He grew up in Kansas and Nebraska, and they planted their crop (wheat, barley, oats, corn, sorghum grain, etc.) and that fall harvested thin crop. In Oregon you had to irrigate all crops to make them grow. It was a big change from a dry land farmer to a irrigated farmer, and he did this change very well.

The railroad that went through our land, when dam was completed they removed the rails from the road bed but left the ties. We picked up all the ties on our place and built a barn. It had 14 stanchions for milk cows—seven cows facing the other seven with five feet between the stanchions to train cows when they came into to be milked. Also it had stalls for the horses. This old barn is still on the place at this time.[2]

While we was in the tent Mom and us kids were digging a basement for a house. As we got deeper in the ground we had to scoop dirt further out as we couldn't throw dirt from hole far enough out and as it was built up would start falling back in the hole. We dug a hole about 16 feet wide and 30 feet long and seven feet deep.

When we got this basement dug I had a long pole and I would pole vault across the basement hole with what I could as my little sister Patty had to try this and she only got halfway and after this she ended up with a broken collarbone.

We had this large early '30s four-door Studebaker car, however rear differential gear was broken so I jacked up with a small little jack and proceeded to unbold the rear end. Back fender where I was working was somewhat sharp on bottom edge of fender. I had a hexagon breaker bar type socket wrench and was removing bolts when the car came off the jack, pinning my right hand under the spring. Under side of fender hit my head, tearing a large chunk of my scalp, laying it down over my ear. Jack ran to house and Mom, Peggy and Pat came out and I told them to place jack and lift car off my hand. They said no and they lifted the car off of me. They tried later and couldn't budge the car. Now Dad took me to Doctor Garison. He was an elderly man and he started working on my head, as it was very dirty from fender. So he started by pouring alcohol, which hurt and I was fighting him and he started cutting my hair on

---
2As of the writing of this book, in 2012.

the torn-loose scalp and I was yelling for him to stop. Dad told the Doc to put me out. He said he's young, he can stand it. Dad told him maybe I could but he couldn't—put him out—besides he needed to set fingers as all four were broken. I held the mask over nose and mouth and Dad applied ether and when I came to I was very sick from ether and aspirin for the hurt in fingers and head. It took 40 to 50 stitches to put my scalp back on. It took some time to heal and grow my hair back.

    I missed baseball season again this year.

Foundations

I was teaching Jack how to walk with your hands on ridge poll in the barn when he fell in the cow manure and knocked him out. I picked him up and headed to the house. We had a 50 gallon barrel buried in the ground. I stopped to wash poop from his face and neck, also started washing his arm, also was yelling for Mom and as they came out I ran my hand down his forearm and it stopped going, making a 90-degree change. I passed out, dropped him into barrel and Mom and Pat pulled him out and threw water on me. Needless to say I caught heck for doing this and many years of teasing from the family and especially Jack. I sure wished he was here today to read this.

When we finally finished foundation, Grandpa Metland helped us to frame up the house and tar paper and ship lap over the paper. The foundation was two feet beyond dirt basement hole we dug. By doing this it cost a lot less than pouring concrete basement, walls and floor.

Dad bought green framing lumber from a small saw mill in Ironside, Oregon. When we say green lumber, a 2x4 was rough-sawed two inches thick and four inches wide, where was today a 2x4, after kiln dried and planed, are now 1.5 inches by 3.5 inches.

I am not sure where they got flooring and shiplap eight inches wide and 3/4 inches thick. They sided the house with that plus tar paper. Studding was in place for the three bedrooms, living room, plus kitchen, but no inter-wall covering. It was wide open inside. We used canvas to cover the windows, used the one door from tent to enter house and basement.

Boy I can't even express the joy the Chard family had as we moved out of that tent, which lasted 2.5 years, and now a house that didn't leak even without windows. Also neighbors all got together and had a house warming—lots of food and coffee, tea, wine, and they had music and had a dance in living room. It was a great time. This would be fall of 1938.

Dad had most of the land was now with crop. He borrowed

money from the bank in Nyssa and bought 20-some head of milk cows. Crops were looking great around the First of July. The main irrigating ditch washed out. This ditch served the entire valley—it was like a large river combined in a large prepared ditch 20 to 25 feet wide and about 15 to 18 feet deep. This main ditch ran around a mountain where the washed out occurred. The CCC boys worked around the clock cutting through the mountain. It took a little over a month to make this repair. So all of the crops without water soon died, and we, like a lot of other farmers, were unable to make payments on time. Bank would not even extend payments so they came to our place and removed all of the milk cows that Dad borrowed money to purchase. Even though they were over half paid for. Needless to say Dad never even used the bank in Nyssa again.

    A new sugar processing plant at Nyssa was built so we started growing sugar beets. Betty, Peggy and myself thinned, hoed the beets. To thin beets you used a 6-inch handle on the hoe, you bent over, separated the beets so there was one beet every seven inches. We received eight dollars an acre. When we hoed them you had a long-handled hoe. We received four dollars per acre. Dad was growing 12 to 15 acres. We didn't get the money until fall. As the folks used money to buy us school clothes, also I would help topping beets. This was done after the fall freeze. You had a large knife with a hook on the end. You would stick the hook into the beet, lift and place beet in other hand, and cut the top off. Throw beet in a winnow. And then pick up beet and throw up into truck bed. We had an old international truck which would hold about eight to 10 ton; this was a wet, muddy backache, miserable job.

    Our farm had many different crops, such as alfalfa that was cut and stacked three times in a year. Litters had to thinned and weeded, then cut each head and placed in a crate, again loaded on truck. Green peas took special mower to cut, then hand loaded the pea vines on truck. Peas were mowed like at daylight and shut down at 10 a.m. Carrot plant seed which grew carrot, we pulled carrots and stored in cellar and at spring we planted the carrots about three inches apart and at fall we go and pull them and cut the stock or the dried up carrot off and put in winnows. When they dried we were ready to combine to retrieve the seed. Onion seed was about like carrot—a two-year crop. Beans you planted about 1.5 inches apart and when the stock produced the bean pods and filled with the bean and when it's at a proper growth, let them dry and combine them.

Before any of these crops were planted the fields were disced, plowed, harrowed and land-planed was also to make field ready to be seeded. Irrigated as the crop grows there is weeding, cultivating, insect spray, all of which must be done to produce a good crop. Think of this when we first came to our place in Oregon, most of this work was done with horses.

In those days if it was daylight, you still had work to do. Although Mom was cleaning up tent and fixing food for next day lunch for us kids when we went to school. I guess I am saying it was a lot of work by all of us to build a new life in this new land in Oregon.

Homesteading

I was in pig heaven when Dad bought a three-wheel case tractor, a small 36 horse engine. We had a hang on one bottom plow, a front and back cultivator, seven-foot mower. We converted disc and harrow to be pulled by the tractor. I was so glad to have it and did most of the tractor work. While I was driving tractor over rough ground I had to stand and bend over, my side would hurt to where it would force me to bend over. The folks would ask why I did this, told them just a little side ache.

We walked two miles to school and back and then Mom said we would go to Sunday school on Sunday. Went some time in summer, again we had to walk two miles to church and two miles home. As the years went by we improved the land and had better crops.

When we went to town we would take egg cases full of eggs, a large can of cream, and Mom would trade this for sugar, flour, cornmeal, salt and pepper. The flour sacks were made of cotton and had different patterns on them. Mom would make things with the clothes like curtains, the girls' underwear. Country girls were teased at school because they wore flour sack panties.

Us kids carried our lunch in a half-gallon tin bucket with a wire bale for a handle. It was rare to have homework as teachers knew we all had miles to walk from school. We finally had a bus. It was 1927 International bus that was used in Chicago in the late '20s and early '30s. It was very old and used and everyone called it "the cracker box," but it was wonderful we didn't have to walk to school anymore.

In 1940 I started high school, both Betty and Peggy several grades ahead of me. Then I guess it was our turn for the mumps. All three girls came down first, then Jack and I just got sick for about six or seven days, throwing up like every hour and it was just green bile. So Mom told Dad to take me to the Doctor, and was drawn over me in fetal position. To the Doctor we went. The Doctor looked me over and told Dad to take me to the hospital. Dad said how much would it cost? Doctor replied your son's life. We went to Ontario and Dad was carrying me up the stairs and my appendix broke and oh it felt so good. And by the time I was on fire they operated and I spent 11 days trying to heal up. Mom stayed with me for some time.

Betty quit high school and married Elver Nielson. He became big brother to me. They lived in Leona, Oregon, and he worked in a lumber mill.

This was wartime and being a farmer, ABC stickers[1] for the car and tractor. This means we could only use so much gasoline; we were able to live with those restrictions. Also sugar and footwear rations. Dad drink hot water and Mom drink coffee. Us kids had hot chocolate. We were milking 20-some head of cows, so we were never short of milk, butter and cheese.

The front tire on the tractor was real bad. We had fixed it at least ten times and finally we was able to find one, had to pay 77 dollars for it. The tire only cost 50 dollars and the balance was what the man at the station wanted and got for getting the tire. I watch the OK Tire Co. take old tires and used a hot tool and cut the grooves in the tire diaper so they would look like they had a better tread then it really had. When ever anything was needed you had to pay extra.

Wartime was tough times. Dad and our neighbor bought a Case IH hay baler together. It was a wire tie type so it took three of us kids to operate the baler and Dad had rented the Bowen land and the Olsen's land, so we had I would guess 90 to 100 acres of hay and

---

1 These referred to rubber and gas rationing mandates put in place in the United States during World War II. An A sticker holder received the lowest gas allocation (3 gallons per week), a B holder received a bit more (8 gallons per week) for what was considered necessary driving, while a C sticker holder received the highest allocation for essential activities. There were no restrictions on this classification (as well as on Class T, for truck drivers, and Class X, including politicians and other "important people"), which was often given to war workers, doctors, police officers and letter carriers (Tony Long, "Dec. 1, 1942: Mandatory Gas Rationing, Lots of Whining," http://www.wired.com/2009/11/1201world-war-2-gasoline-rationing/ (November 30, 2009)). For more information on gas rationing and to view images of wartime ration books, see "World War II Rationing on the U.S. Homefront," (http://www.ameshistory.org/exhibits/events/rationing.htm), "Your Car is a War Car Now," (http://www.prewarbuick.com/features/your_car_is_a_war_now), and "Gas Rationing WWII," (http://envisioningtheamericandream.com/2012/11/15/gas-rationing-wwii/).

stacked all of the bales of hay. The stacks was 24 bales wide plus two bales high. They could lift the bales up to 12 bales high and carry them up after that to 24 bales high, and the stack was a couple hundred feet long. When Dad sold hay that fall, each bale averaged out at 113 pounds. I weighed 102 pounds and missed a lot of school because I had to work at home. I should inject here when I was 12 I drove derrick team[2] lifting loose hay up on hay stack. Ten-hour day and they fed us at noon. I received 50 cents a day. Oh yes. I thinned 20 acres lettuce for a long-legged bay mare. I didn't know till later she had been bitten by a rattlesnake and believe me she could go sideways even when running, and you're on the ground.

It was in my sophomore year five or six of us rode up in the hills looking for deer. It was quite cool and we rose up to a shale type cliff. It was 60 to 70 feet down of loose shale rock. One of the guys was riding a stud horse and it bit my mare on her butt and she jumped forward right over the cliff. When we hit into the shale she couldn't keep her feet under her, and I couldn't get out of saddle, so she rolled over me before we slide to the bottom and I was out of my breath, and if I had a gun in my hands I would have shot her. I felt like I had water in my boots. It wasn't water, it was blood, as the saddle horn poked a small hole in my stomach. I tried to use my left hand, the hand was going in the wrong way and then I saw it was broken and the bone was sticking out of the skin about one and a half inches, bleeding some. By then the guys got there and wrapped arm and my stock and headed home. It was 17 miles; believe me it felt like 100 miles. When I got home Mom and Dad were gone and it just happened that my Uncle drove in and he took me to the Doctor,

---

2 A system in which men would use pitchforks to sling bales of hay into horse drawn sloops or sleighs and hoist them onto the top of the stack with a boom stacker. Later systems would use cables and pulleys connecting to the horses' harnesses, raising a large wooden arm that would toss the bales onto the top of the stack (Mack Bryson, "Running a Ranch," in A Cowboy's Life (Victoria, BC, Canada: FriesenPress, 2013) p. 34).

who set my arm, and it was in a cast above my elbow down over my wrist, and a couple of inches in my stomach.

    We had combined the grain on the Olsen place and the grain was in the field in sacks about 80 pounds each. They had to be picked up in the field and taken to a steel grainery. Dad hurt his knee and wasn't feeling well, so Jack and I took the truck and went up to field to pick up grain. I couldn't lift the sacks, they would slip out, so Jack and I wrapped the cast with barb wire around lower arm and it would grip sacks real well, and we completed the job in two days. Jack would drive truck to the sacks and I would buck them up on the truck. When loaded, I would drive to grainery and dump them, as Dad wanted to save sack for future use.

    The Idaho Power Company was putting line in most of the farm roads. The farmers would dig the holes for the power poles and oh what wander when we got electric lights. A neighbor wired our house and barn and hard light. It took some time to get a refrigerator, electric stove and 15-gallon hot water tank and finally a Philco radio. I have to admit that I wondered if I turned radio on and the song would start, but if some one else turned theirs on an hour later would they start the same song back up to match when we turned ours on? But when we got it, I found out how it worked. It was real dumb on my part, but I never was around anything like that. We would listen to *Ma Perkins*[3] at noontime, at night listen to *I Love a Mystery*[4] and several others, and the war news of which I could not wait to join the service.

    I hunted a lot with a .22 rifle and shot small birds, ground squirrels and many jackrabbits. And I started hunting pheasants with Dad's old 10-gauge shotgun and I swear it wounded in front and killed behind. To explain to our younger ones today, the shotgun

---

[3] One of the most famous and successful radio soap operas of all time, Ma Perkins aired as a daytime daily serial from 1933 to 1960, culminating in 7,065 episodes in its 27 year run. Visit https://archive.org/details/MaPerkins021950 to listen to a selection of Ma Perkins episodes.

[4] A radio adventure-mystery serial drama that aired from 1939 to 1953 and followed the exploits of three mystery seeking crime solvers. Visit https://archive.org/details/otr_iloveamystery to listen to a selection of I Love a Mystery episodes.

was lightweight and when you shot it kicked back so hard you was almost knocked down. Nevertheless a dog we had at the time was always with me while hunting and when we finally shot one it fell and I was jumping up and down and the dog ran and caught it so I only broke a wing and brought it back and it was tickled as I was, wagging its tail and jumping up and down. I did improve thereafter, however one day we were hunting, the dog and I, and we saw a pheasant across the ditch from us. Well I cocked the shotgun and the dog and I jumped across the ditch. As I landed I somehow pulled the trigger and it kicked back hitting me in the stomach and I landed back down in the ditch. It was about two feet deep. The dog jumped in, drug me out of the water and went to the house for dry clothes and Mom saw me and wanted to know what happened. I told her and she told Dad to get his boy a good shotgun, so he talked my uncle out of his double barrel 16-gauge Star Leader shotgun with long 32-inch barrels. I loved this old gun, which was made by a Boston Cycle Co., Boston, Massachusetts. Not trying to brag, but my cousins came out from Kansas and we all went hunting—at that time each person was allowed four birds. There was six of us hunting in a beet field and we only had my dog, but he hunted all across the beet field, but the pheasants were always in front of me. I shot 24 times and killed 24 pheasants. Needless to say I took a ribbing from all of them that day.

 I believe Steve Chard still has this old gun—he was going to repair or put a new stock on it. He gave me a 12-gauge shotgun and I gave that gun to Ryan Chard. That ended my shotgun days.

 I had joined the C.A.P. Civil Air Patrol.[5] We were taugh many

---

5 The Civil Air Patrol was created in the late 1930s (one week before the Japanese attack on Pearl Harbor) in response to the calls of over 150,000 volunteer aviators lobbying for a way to apply their skills toward national defense. Under the jurisdiction of the Army Air Corps, CAP volunteers sunk two enemy submarines during World War II and saved hundreds of crash victims. After the war, CAP was incorporated as a nonprofit organization, and continues to promote aerospace education, cadet programs, and emergency response services as a

things, such as first aid, articles of war and we were told that they would teach us to fly. But always something came up and all kind of excuses why they couldn't get airplanes to teach us. I quit and I knew that I wanted to join the service and Mom and Dad were against my joining the service. I sent for and received my brother's birth certificate, but I was sure they wouldn't believe I was that old. Finally Mom agreed to sign papers to let me join. I enlisted in Ontario, Oregon, and they sent me to Portland, Oregon, where they gave everyone a complete physical and turned me down and gave me a ticket home. I was sure the Marines would take me, but Mom said, "No, we go to Boise, Idaho and enlist in the Navy." I was accepted in the USNR and would be called up for duty in a short time. I was 16 at that time.

---

civilian auxiliary organization to the U.S. Air Force today. For more information, visit http://www.gocivilairpatrol.com.

THE WAR YEARS

I AM SOMEWHAT at a loss to write down what I saw and what I did. I'll start when I was called up. I report at Boise Train Depot and we would ride train to San Diego. There were 14 people all from Idaho, Oregon and Washington. My family was all there—Mom, Dad, Jack and Pat. Dad lifted me up on steps of the rail car and he said, "You are just a boy going to do a man's job; you do that and if you are killed you die like a man as well."

Boot camp you learned many things. You did a lot of running, all kinds of shots, marching, swimming. We had to jump from tower with a life jacket at 25 feet and then 50 feet. After that we were shown how to stay afloat with your pants and other items. Also they poured oil in a pool and set it on fire. We again jumped into pool from 25-foot tower and removed life jacket, dive down and when you needed air you would splash water above you and go up for air and swim under water to end of pool. I was scared stiff but I did it. We walked 17 miles on the beach with a wood rifle and a 60-pound backpack. We had a two-man tent with a ground cloth, one wool blanket, and of course sea rations. For dinner they toss each one of us a sea ration box. I was lucky and my ration had a small can of beans and bacon, four crackers, four cigarettes. That was dinner. Next morning we were up and backpacks packed by 5:30 a.m. and we walked about a mile and had sea rations again. We were shown how to shoot 20 and 40-millimeter guns, load fire them, load them and remove barrels when they got too hot. We spent the day there, marched back to base.

We were shown how to fight fire onboard ship. A large metal ship was set in concrete and the lower part of ship had oil in it. A four man team would enter one end of ship with fire hose and put the fire out. We were wearing mask with oxygen as it was cool on you face and breathing, and you could be blistering. After fire was out you had to walk full length of ship in the black smoke and believe me you could not see nothing so you would touch hand rail, which was very hot, and try to hold your breath as long as you could, and when we came out the other end we were crying from the smoke and coughing. Our faces were black from the smoke and that was a very tough day.

When returned to base we had rifle training, hand grenades and poison gas training. The full company went to the rifle range and I still was quite small, like 5 feet 4 inches tall and maybe 105 pounds. Anyway, we were issued 30-oz bolt-action rifles and we were shooting 300 yards a 6-inch bullseye. You shot five times standing, of which I had three shots in bullseye; then five shots kneeling and I had four shots in bullseye; then 10 shots prone and I had nine shots in bullseye and last shot cut the edge of the bullseye and the gun I had a loose rear sight and each time I shot it would move as first shot was low on left side of bullseye and by the 10th shot they had worked its way across and cut the edge in upper righthand corner. This then sent me and one other sailor to the marine base for further shooting, all of which was prone shooting. I was issued another rifle; 300 yards, ten shots all in bullseye; 600 yards, nine in bullseye and one close miss; 900 yards, only three in bullseye and at 900 yards a 9-inch bullseye looked like a pin head. But Navy issued me a rifle expert medal.[1]

Hand grenade training was a structure that stood three stories high and had openings representing windows and doors. And on each side as a trench about 3 feet wide, 4 feet deep, with a dirt mound 2 to 3 feet high facing the structure. The dummy hand grenades were the shape and weight of the real thing and we were taught to take a stand legs apart and throw the grenades through the lower windows of structure, then throw through second-story windows, which was very easy for me to do, so they told me to [throw] through the third

---

1 This medal was then called a Navy Expert Rifleman Medal (since 1969 it has been referred to as a Navy Rifle Marksmanship Medal) and is the highest possible commendation of its kind, more prestigious than the lower and midrange "marksman" and "sharpshooter" qualifying levels below it. For more information, visit http://www.medalsofamerica.com/Item--i-F074_Full_Size_List.

story of which I did, and the guys in the trench on the other side were yelling as it was landing in their trench.

Gas training was tear gas and clip that changed color in presence of gas.

After four weeks we had our first pass to go to town. What I did first: went to a cleaners where they did sewing and had them cut my dress uniform to fit me, as they gave us all larger uniforms. Some of us ended up at the old sail ship called the Silver Star where we bought my first beer, which I thought was terrible. Also I smoked my first cigarette.

Peggy Chard and another girl from Nyssa was working in a war plant in Los Angeles area and John Gernhardt and I went up there and visited Peggy and John's older sister. I stayed all night with Peggy and she told me what bus to catch to meet John. Anyway, I took the wrong bus to catch to meet John and ended up in the wrong place. I knew I had to get back to base so I took the A train, which went to San Diego and made it back to base on time. John was already there and he said where the hell was I as he didn't think he would ever see me again and I ended up in a rough neighborhood.

Our company turn came up for one week in kitchen. We peeled the potatoes, broke the eggs, mashed the potatoes, washed tables, put all trays, cups, etc. in dishwasher, then place them ready for next meal. We eat last. We served about 640 people in this mess hall and I believe there was four of them. Anyway, it was good to be done with that. Our chief who was over our company felt a young ensign[2] was riding us a little too hard while in parade, so he marched up to the stand, went up the ladder and confronted the ensign and they had words and the chief knocked the ensign off of the stand.

Needless to say we never saw that chief again. A few days later, with completing boot camp, we all received 10 days leave plus five days travel time. John and I traveled together. When we got to Salt Lake we had to change buses. We were in a line of 45 to 50 people. This man from the bus company asked John and I for our tickets and then he came back and told us to go outside, get on a bus and duck

---
2 An officer of the lowest rank in the U.S. Navy.

Basic mileage ration, 1942. By Office of Price Administration. [Public domain], via Wikimedia Commons.

USS YMS 65, 1943. Reprinted with permission courtesy of Vetfriends.com.

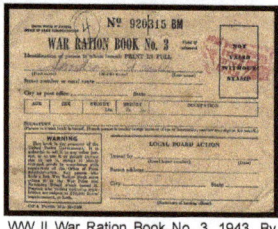

WW II War Ration Book No. 3, 1943. By Bill Faulk. [Public domain], via Wikimedia Commons.

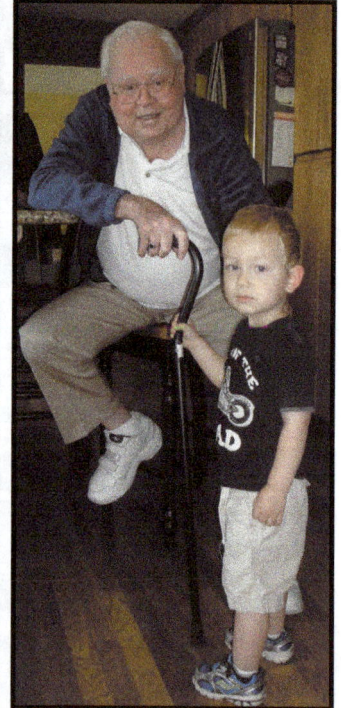

down so no one could see us and we were on our way. If we had to wait in that line, we would have missed that bus and wait until after next day. Rode bus to Caldwell, Idaho and again change buses. About 8-hour wait so we walked to highway and hitched a ride with a Naval officer going to Portland. John talked him into going to Nyssa instead, through New Plymouth and Ontario, to Vale. This saved him many miles as there were no freeways in those days.

Had wonderful time at home. Mom cooked all of my favorite foods. I dated a few girls while home and hated to leave. Betty and Elver and Mary and Bill also saw me off.

Returned to San Diego and I was sent to Camp Elliot, California, was offered two choices: Seabees[3] or sea duty. I took sea duty and was told to get ready to ship out.

I should say I wasn't the only one in the family that was in the service. My cousins as follows also served during World War II: Earl Fox, USN radio man and spent war in Washington; Bob Tallot, medic, Pacific area; Farrel Kusniski, USA killed in Europe. Delmar Metland, USA in California; Kenneth Chard, USNR Pacific Theater.

The following I pretty well kept bottled up inside of me as I didn't want my mother and others to know what I saw and did. Also I did not cry, Dad, no matter how bad it was. And believe me as I write this I can now cry at last. War is a hell. I hope to explain the horror and horrifying experience that happened to a 17-year-old. I aged ten years in a very short time. And people reading books talking about the glory of war are plain idiots.

I will start here as I received shots at Camp Elliot, issued rifle and other gear and marched down to docks. Red Cross was there giving us coffee and donuts as we boarded this barge AKA transport

---

3 A Naval Construction Battalion program established after the attack on Pearl Harbor in 1941, to support the Navy and Marines in remote locations by building bases and developing military infrastructure, as well as defend itself in the event of an enemy attack. For more information, visit http://www.seabeesmuseum.com/history.html.

ship.[4] My bunk was number four in 8-high—if you wanted to turn over you slid out and turned over, slid in again. I was told there were 3,000 of us on board. It was January or February of 1944.

We went down to chow the eve of the day we loaded and had just finished eating and went up on deck and watched the tugboat bump up against the ship and oh boy I was sick—hadn't left the dock and went to my bunk and stayed there for four days getting up to throw up in bathroom. They had large 20 gallon cans for us to be sick in.

Fourth day another sailor gave me bread and my seasickness was over. When you are seasick you feel every movement of the ship makes, and when you are over seasickness the sky and sea move, not the ship. We were in at least 24 convoy. First stop was Wake Island.[5] We all had to wear helmets and our rifles and go over side of ship on landing nets into landing craft and headed to shore where we waded to shore, dove into trenches. We were pretty slow in our first try so we went to ship and did it all over again, improving, then again at Mary's, Anna's, and Carolina islands.[6] I am not sure now which islands were first now, but we practiced unloading and to the beaches into trenches as before at Wake Island.

Next stop was Luzon, Philippines. Before we got there a mine floated up and exploded quite near our ship. When it exploded I was

---

4 Attack Cargo Ship.
5 It's possible that either the timeline is off here, or these events took place at a different island, as Wake Island was controlled by the Japanese after it was overtaken from a small band U.S. Marines and civilian defenders in the Battle of Wake Island in December 1941, and remained under Japanese control until the end of the war in 1945 ("Battle of Wake Island," http://www.britannica.com/event/Battle-of-Wake-Island).
6 It's likely that Mary's Island most likely refers to current day Kanton Island (originally named Mary Ballcout's Island, and as known as Canton Island and Abariringa Island). It is the only inhabited island of the Phoenix Islands, which are a part of independent Republic of Kiribati, an atoll located approximately halfway between Hawaii and Figi in the South Pacific (http://www.mashpedia.com/Kanton_Island). A record of Anna's Island was not available. Carolina Island likely refers to the Caroline Islands, a archipelago in the western Pacific Ocean. The islands were fortified by the Japanese prior to World War II, and in 1944 the United States gained control over the atoll (http://ww2db.com/country/Caroline%20Islands and http://www.britannica.com/place/Caroline-Islands).

watching, leaning against an open hatch and was blown over hatch and fell 27 feet down onto a wooden hatch top on the lower deck. I was unconscious and was taken to sickbay, came to and was taken released to go back to my bunk.

We are now anchored at Luzon Bay and sailors were being transferred to other ships. My name came up and I was to report to the upper deck and this little wooden ship pulled alongside and two of us were lowered to this little ship and the people said welcome to USS YMS 65. I was advised and was requested because of my rifle expert medal class as a radar operator. We sailed with several other ships heading to Manila, Philippines. I believe it took us two days. Once there the crew wanted to get a record player and speakers, so they talked the skipper to drop depth charges and we gathered up all kinds of fish and sold them to the people on the docks. So now we could have music throughout the ship. The Navy gave us many records of songs of that time, also big band music.

The ship was resupplied, getting to move out in a large convoy. We were to pick up food at a large cement floating food storage unit. As we approached an 8-inch steel pipe extended out about 20 feet or so and the tide caught us and we slammed into the steel pipe. It hit first on pilot house, which was steel-plated. Ship was still moving forward, then it hit the railing to pilot house, tearing it off, hitting 20-millimeter gun, breaking gun from mount. Steel arm broke open a 50-gallon barrel of gasoline, which ignited and was burning and spilled down on deck and we were still moving forward. It poked a hole in the first smoke stack and slicing a slot across the second stack, continuing, and tore the tent over back of ship off. We put the fire out and picked up our food, both fresh and frozen, canned good, etc. We headed for shipyards for repairs. They worked the rest of that day and all night and we were ready to sail. I didn't know where we were going, but found out much later.

Being one of the youngest aboard I stood many different posts, such as lookouts on starboard and port side, telegraph, radar and helm. I should tell you when I was instructed as to steer the ship and how you steer by compass, so like a real greenhorn, I said, 'Oh goody I get to drive,' and boy I was teased about that. Also they wanted to know if I was a hick, so I ask what was a hick. They said anybody from a town less than 25,000 population. I told them and was many hicks because Nyssa, Oregon had only 1,200 to 1,500 people. One other man was from Los Angeles, California and all other personnel were from east of Mississippi River. They never heard of Oregon, only in school, and wondered if we had Indian problems and if we had cement sidewalks because western movies showed dirt streets and wooden sidewalks. They were surprised of the many modern things we had out there in the West.

Well I found where we were going—Saipan[7] in the chain of islands leading to Japan. Convoy was 50 or so ships. Battle ships line up at 10 to 15 miles off shore, then a row of cruisers, then destroyers and destroyer escorts, then came the AKA transport ships loaded with Marines. Oh yes, there were aircraft carriers out there as well. Then there were LSI[8] and LST[9] large landing craft, and there were cargo ships and many others. When aircraft started bombing and the brigs ships started shelling the shore, we are sent in to sweep the landing area of shallow mines and talk about noise, all of these ships and supplies for the Marines who are going to go ashore.

It seemed to me that Japanese could not shoot out at battle ships, which pissed them off and they would shoot at us and other closer ships. You could hear the 16-inch shells go over us and they would sound like a train going over, like swoosh, swoosh, then on in and explode. We had many holes in ship, but no one was hurt.

When the minesweepers completed we were sent to other areas in the various inlets of deeper mines laid for larger ships and subs. Marines were advancing toward the higher ground. The Japanese had convinced a lot of the natives that the Americans would rape the women and their children, so many of them went to a 50 to 100-foot cliff and throw their children over and then they would jump them-

---

[7] For more information on the Battle of Saipan, which took place on June 15, 1944, see the History Channel coverage: http://www.history.com/topics/world-war-ii/battle-of-saipan.
[8] Landing Ship, Infantry.
[9] Landing Ship, Tank.

selves. It was a horrifying site I will never ever forget.

I know certain sounds trigger nerves and you jump out of your hide, plus brings back things you try to hide. It was my first time people trying to kill us or blow us out of the water. I stood starboard watch to look for any mines came up close to us. None did. But when we sweep the deeper mines in entrance to the docks, lots of them popped up and we were assigned as the gunship to blow mines as they were cut loose and floated to surface.

Generally we would use only 20's, 50's and 30's guns, not the three-inch-long barrel cannon. There was a man much older than I. He was shooting the 20-millimeter gun. There was about 10 mines and he had shot over 100 rounds and had hit nothing. So I was told to take over that gun. I shot and blew three mines with only 22 shells. I was assigned that gun from then on.

I will try to explain how we swept mines. You put your gear out. First a float shaped like a barrel with a rounded nose and tail fins. It had a place on top for a pole and flag. A cable was attached underneath in various links, like 20, 30, 40, 50 feet long. However deep, we were to sweep the other end of the cable from the float to a outer. It was a metal square with curved blades shaped to pull down and out from the ship. The float with the length of cable below float would hold the other device at required level. As the cable was extended out, they attached a block on the cable which held an explosive cable cutter. These were placed 30 to 40 feet apart as the other pulled the cable out from the ship. Generally around three to four hundred feet, then inner unit was attached and lowered on the main cable to same levels as the cable attached to the float. So as the ship moved forward you were pulling the cable and float would be at a angle away from ship, the float somewhat behind the ship, like 20 to 30 yards. And when the mine came up against cable and slid down and hit, the explosive charge would cut it and it would float to surface.

First ship through was at a greater risk as they could hit shallower mines. Second ship and all that followed, they would follow in areas being sweep ahead of them. Always the threat of a mine slow to float for whatever reason and hit your ship, so all eyes were watching the waters ahead of you in hopes that none hit your ship. I believe only one minesweeper was lost in Saipan.

After the invasion was pretty well over, I still had to go ashore to headquarters for mail and orders. It was raining hard. There were four of us, so we were given a four-wheel Dodge Power Wagon, canvas top, no doors or side curtains and we got stuck in the mud. It was like wall to wall quagmire. We were wet, cold, muddy and what were we to do? Walk out of that mud was impossible for for us to walk. Getting dark and no traffic, there happened to be a large power shovel with a good size cab and engine compartment. I started the diesel engine, warmed the cab and compartments where we spent the night. Next morning sun was shining and steam was coming up from the ground everywhere you looked. Traffic started moving and a big truck pulled us out. Caught heck on ship for being gone 24 hours overdue. Wasn't much I could have done and finally they agreed.

We were now being restocked with food, repairs and replacement of personnel of those showing stress. I'm not sure how this was done.

We are to join a large convoy heading where I did not know where. We were in the group heading for Okinawa, the last of the big islands before Japan. They had been there for some time and was well prepared for the invasion. We sweep the landing area without too much shelling of the minesweepers. This was the worst fight the marines had; I heard and later confirmed that they lost over 50,000 marines—their largest loss of life in the island hopping process for the marines.

We did not stay long there, as we were sent to Formosa, now known as Taipan.[10] This turned out to be a hellhole for us. The Chinese were there, but the Imperial Japanese were also there. We tied up at their large inlet for supplies and fuel. Oil tender pumped all of

---

10 He was likely referring to Taiwan, known then as Portuguese Formosa, and it's capital city of Taipei (Ginsberg, N. Taiwan. In Encyclopaedia Britannica Online. http://www.britannica.com/place/Taiwan).

the oil up the hill in large storage tanks. Chinese soldiers refused to protect our fuel. Also there were about 100 suicide Japanese boats that they did not want to guard, so we were elected to protect our fuel. Each ship furnished so many people to stand guard on oil tanks and boats, as well as required aboard ship. All minesweepers only had a crew of 21 to 29 people, including the four officers aboard. So the ship was shorthanded as all guard spent at least 12-hour shifts not only on guard duty, but aboard ship. People were tired and accidents happened all due to stress and tiredness. First big problem was our turn for all night guard of oil storage. There was four of us all armed and as we approached the tanks one fellow was shot and killed, so only the three of us stood guard in dugout foxholes. Around 2 a.m. someone kept yelling "Joe, I need help," and we had no one by that name, as they could not get a fix on the rest of us. Soon after our turn came up to guard the suicide boats. One of the guards was rather husky and during the night the Japanese opened up in hopes to blow them. Well this fellow dove into a culvert and became stuck. We finally heard him yelling and we had a small guy crawl in and tie a rope around feet and greased the walls, pulled him out backwards, skinned up some. The kidding started right there and many laughs. It was great to laugh, which broke up the stress we were under.

    There were many sunken ships, ferries, barges, etc., some were still sticking up out of water at various angles. So now the Japanese would hide in these old sunken ships and ferries, etc. At night they would swim by our ships and throw hand grenades aboard, and now another problem to deal with—someone saw somebody on one of these so a search was set up. Soon after dark we went out to search the old sunken ships and ferries. I was along with another sailor. He had a bolt action .30-06 rifle. I had a Thompson submachine gun, a drum of shells and four clips.

    We had just stepped aboard a ferry at an angle. The part sticking out was the pilot house and wheel house, all made of thin plywood. So the gun I had was a .45-caliber. The first shot hit the sailor beside me, but he did not fall into water. He was hit in stomach and pushed him against the inner wall. I got behind a large steel post and whenever I saw a flash from them I filled the area with bullets. The boat with help was on their way back to us. By then I had emptied the drum of shells and all four clips. I grabbed the dropped rifle and kept on shooting till it was empty of all five rounds.

They all were there now to help. They searched the ferry and no one was left alive. There was many, many Japanese was killed. They had returned fire and bullets went through the steel post frontside, only dimpled the backside and I must have been real close as I had a black eye swollen shut, a large bruise on jaw and body and leg. They took me back to my ship and the wounded man to a doctor on a destroyer. I was a mess. I have lived with this now for many years and those 10 to 12 minutes are still in my dreams and thoughts every damn day and I am thankful to be here.

The men on ship, including the captain, asked what happened on the ferry. The lieutenant that was with us came back to our ship and told skipper what he saw and what I did. I drank the whiskey like water and didn't sleep for two days. They finally gave me a shot as I couldn't sleep. It's out in the open now and I have asked the good Lord to help me live with this.

So we weren't done yet with mines, so we sweeping other areas for many days and shipping inlets. One evening coming into a large bay with many ferries operating in this bay, a suicide boat popped out, missing our ship as we both going same direction, and headed direct towards a large ferry loaded with people. We could not shoot as we would be hitting the ferry or other ships. The suicide boat was going about 45 miles an hour. It hit the ferry in the center and blew up. Parts of ferry blow 50 feet or better in the air and people everywhere. We helped by pulling mostly wounded people onboard. Many boats came to help. The water turned red with blood from the dead and injured. Body parts was everywhere, one of the worst horrifying sites you could ever imagine.

The war is near its end. We have endured two invasions, two

typhoons and still afloat—time was flying by, but at times it nearly drags. I tired to stay busy, as on small ships you got to do a lot of different tasks. One day making fresh water from salt water, repairing ropes, cables, repair railings and learned how to splice ropes, make fenders out of rope. I learned how to splice high tension cable both left hand right hand twist, so work was seldom completed. Storms raised heck with us while trying to sweep a given area.

We are short handed as our Pharmacist's father died so they flew him home. Also some showed stress and they were sent to other jobs on ships that were not so stressful. (Will explain stress later).

We are now heading to China and the Yellow Sea, which is mud from the River Yangtze,[11] which is one of the largest in China. As we are approaching the Wang Po River to go up to Shanghai, China, we tangle with a Japanese gunboat. He was way outclassed and had small guns, so we captured it and put it behind our ship and in front of the other minesweeper with guards aboard. Destroyer had us come alongside and there transferred admiral and his staff aboard and we were to get him up the river to Shanghai for plans to meet with General Shang-pshic[12] and his wife, present rulers of China. Also this is now August 30th or 31st. War is over. Wow what a wonderful feeling. No more shooting, but someone hadn't removed all of the mine fields. But now we were taking an admiral to Shanghai.

You go up the Wang Po River and in China the Chinese junk ships, some close to 80 feet long, would turn and cut across in front of a power boat as it would remove all evil spirits and they would have good luck.

Well this [ship], oh boy, about 80 feet or so long waited a bit long and we were going to hit him right in the middle of his junk. So the helmsman turned ship a full 90 degrees left and had engines

---

11 The River Yangtze is in fact the largest river in both China and Asia, and the third largest river in the world, spanning some 3,915 miles (Greer, C. Yangtze River. In Encyclopaedia Britannica Online. http://www.britannica.com/place/Yangtze-River).

12 No reference to this general could be found, however it's likely he was referring to Chiang Kai-shek, the head of China's Nationalist government from 1928 to 1949 (Chiang Kai-shek. In Encyclopaedia Britannica Online. http://www.britannica.com/biography/Chiang-Kai-shek).

in full reverse, even as small as we were, does not stop and back up. It takes a good number of feet for this to happen. As we headed for the bank with a four or 5-foot cement wall at the top, we finally got her stopped and as she was nearing the bank we hit muddy banks and ships bow kept rising up. When she stopped we could step onto the cement wall from our bow. She was stuck in the mud. So unload small motorboat we carried and took mine cable from winch on starboard side, putting a large grappling hook on cable, taking out about 50 yards at a 20 to 30 percent angle from ship, hopped into river bottom. Same was done on port side. With engine in reverse we would pull ship one way and then the other about one half hour we got her out of the mud. I have no idea what the skipper was telling the admiral. By now there is thousands of people lining the banks of the river, waving, yelling, waving flags. It was something to see and I will never forget it. Also on that trip up the river we counted 18 dead babies, and would say most were baby girls, as we found out that the boat people wanted to keep only boys because they could work. Also we counted eight elderly people. They just roll them into river when they pass away.

We think this is terrible, but only a way of life for them.

We deposit the admiral in nice hotel and we get our first leaves, like 24 hours. We were advised to stay in groups of five as Japanese were still around.

I was one of the first to go, like all sailors, we went to base and tried to see Shanghai from the inside of bars. This I was not familiar with and did not like. I did enjoy the music and dancing. I met this white Russian girl and we danced a lot, drink a little and the first thing I knew it was 2 a.m. and the bar was closing and I was alone. She lived above bar. I had no idea where I was and ask her to tell rickshaw driver where I wanted to return to my ship. So off I went and some of the side streets are very narrow, so we went down several and came out on a main drag and the Chinese were escorting Japanese soldiers, were being taken to a ship to be transported back to Japan. A young Japanese officer who spoke English wondered where I was going. I told him and he join us—we're going right by your ship. He had attended school in California at one time. So I was delivered safe and sound back to my ship by the enemy.

Speaking of this heard from Mom and Dad at last only a couple of letters, but oh what a boast to me they said everyone was well and what they were doing. Dad had sold all milk cows Saturday after I left Monday. I knew that's why he had me, to milk his cows. Also they were building an internment camp at Nyssa and German prisoners of war confined there and they used them as farm labor workers. Dad even used them to thin and hoe sugar beets.

We could now tell folks where we were and what we were doing. During war we could not write letters to anyone and tell them what you do or doing, where you were or where you were going, not even if it was dark. Your letters said hello and how they were was always great to hear from them. If you said anything about where you are, or hurt, etc., they just blacked out so they received no news from me.

What is stress and when it was time to be referred, some slept all the time, would fall asleep eating, could not stand their watch. Others talked loud generally to themselves. Some would cry or stutter.

Many different problems come up when a mine pops in front of your ship. You better have men wide awake and know what to do when this happens. We have had minesweeper blow right in front of us—not saying person was not doing his job and didn't know, but the war is over, other ships going home and we're still here trying to clean up someone else's mess. We are trying to clean up the mouth of Wang Po and where the Yangtze dumps into Yellow Sea. We would sweep with mine and magnetic. Magnetic mines do not have cable, they come when a ship comes over them, creating a magnetic field and the mine would come up and blow the ship. All American ships had a unit that demagnetized the ship called degaussing. And we would complete our sweep and later some damn fool would not turn theirs on and boom, another ship was hit—maybe not sunk, but people hurt.

As the rivers change channels almost daily with all the silt and mud from these rivers, so back we would go and sweep some more. One night the destroyer invited us sweepers to a new movie and they came and picked whoever wanted; one other and myself went over. When it got dark, as the movie was on the fantail, well it decided to have a weather change, wind blowing rain in sheets, so movie was cancelled and they were going to take us back to our ships. We were anchored in the mouth of Wang Po River and as we went by, letting some off of the whale boat, I think there were six or seven aboard beside the two crewmen. All of sudden we hit a large wave and our little whale boat was full of water and rolled over. We did have life jackets on, as the other sailor from ship and I came out on leeward side of boat, so we decided to stay with the upside down boat. Some of the ships weren't far, but they did not know we sank and how are you going to get aboard if ladder was not still hanging? So we hung on and floated down the river. About 4 a.m. it quit blowing and raining and when it was light there was no ships in sight. It was a long, long, long night, and now no help anywhere in sight. I thought they hadn't blown us up yet, so now they going to drown me. Not too comforting thoughts. But we still hung on. About noon an airplane spotted us and we were picked up about 2 p.m. I never went to another movie on another ship unless we were tied up. It took about a week for us to wear out the wrinkles in our hands and feet, and about that long to quit shaking.

Once again we were on the move again. This time to Hong Kong. We only refueled there and we were heading to the archipelago islands below Singapore.[13] We sweep mines in various parts there. Now we're headed to Sasebo, Japan. It's winter time. I'm sick with laryngitis. I could not talk and was still standing my watch on radar as now I was the only one that knew how to operate it. So my watch was 8 p.m. to 8 a.m. Since I couldn't talk, I would write down info and they had a deckhand stand 4-hour shifts with me and they relaid info to the bridge. Ship was covered with ice. Seas were rough

---
13 Ken spelled Singapore "Sing a poor".

and wind was in the 40 to 50 mile-an-hour range. It was not easy to heat ship in this weather. But lots of clothes helped. I slept in the day time and sick of eating sea rations. We finally arrived in Sasebo, Japan. This was their submarine base. Several large subs still there and many two-man subs. How anyone could stand to even get in one of these is beyond anything I could imagine. Weather has calmed down in this large port. We did sweep where they said mines were laid, but we found none.

We borrowed a truck from Army and 12 of us drove to Nagasaki, Japan, where the second Atomic Bomb was dropped. It blew up above the ground like about 500 to 800 feet above the ground and to see the total destruction of this bomb is unbelievable. Your first view there is nothing left to see, only piles of broken stone and brick. I would say total destruction in a 7 mile circle. Directly where it blew the ground was bare and burnt look, about 3,000 yards circle. On one end some twisted steel beams and heavy metal was all bent and bent away from the center where bomb went off. Glass windows were little puddles of melted glass laying here and there. Trees that were two to three feet thick at base and now stood six to seven feet high, was charred from 12 to 8 inches in front or facing center where bomb blew, and to my amazement the backside new little twigs have come out with leaves.

On an arched bridge made of concrete, a cart being pulled by a small burrow and a man sitting in cart—this imprint was left on that bridge's deck. A large building further up on hill, like three or four miles, the front of this building was gone. Destruction everywhere you looked. Any person or animal was completely evaporated. I took many pictures and later I mailed home. We spent the day in that area, where bomb blew large steel mills, large type brick buildings, all completely destroyed. Nothing was left that had any shape, that even appeared as a building, just a pile of broken brick, melted glass. This part of town was above the coastal town. That area was still standing. However many people that was warned to clear out of the area, but most did not take this and now they were burned, eyes melted when trying to see the bomb. The fortunate people are the ones that were killed, as the after affect was pure hell.

I wanted to feel bad for these people, but somehow the two invasions at Saipan and Okinawa, I was still very bitter and why they wanted to rule the Pacific and the United States. I was ready to go home. After returning to the ship we had orders to prepare and refit and fuel up. We were going home.

Before finishing this, I should get a few more things out in the open, at least in my mind as they been bottled up inside of me long enough, and since I finally started writing down the war years. I am not sure where this happened, but the first one happened when we were sweeping and a large mine about 70 to 80 feet away blew up and this sailor was standing on deck when it went off. He was cut in half, top half went overboard and lower lay on deck, kicking. As I had deck duty, this sight made me and many others sick. Now I and the Pharmacist had to sew him in canvas with lead weight for burial at sea. This was damn hard to do and the top half was never found. What happened to this man really affected me—anger, yes, and a new insight that I could fight back with every ounce of strength in me.

The next one happened where the mine tangled or hooked onto something and broke, when this steel cable broke. When this happens the loose end flies back like a whip, smashing whatever was in its path. This time took out six feet of the gunnel, which is made up of four-by-six oak upright posts and 1.5-inch plywood sides. Cable was repaired and gear replaced and we got back in line and no sooner than we started and we snagged up again, and again line came flying back, took out more railing. One piece hit me on my left thigh, did break the skin, only bruised—that I wore for close to a year. The cable wrapped around this sailor his chest and one arm, and the cable was unwinding, tear the meat and muscle on his chest and arm. We had to wrap cable with copper wire on each side of the cable before cutting. The Pharmacist gave him morphine and he sat there and smoked and talked, telling us about his wife and twins. You could not believe the arm and hand was contorted into a gross shape. But the muscle being wrapped in the cable, it took us close two hours to free him. We went to the destroyer and hoisted him aboard, as they had a doctor. We never saw him again.

There were many little accidents, bumps and bruises. Lots of boring hours you never knew if it was your turn to be hurt or killed. Also, a rather funny incident that happened, we received shipments of dehydrated potatoes, carrots, red beets. They were sealed in five-gallon square cans, of which were stored with cargo rope ladder in front of galley, which was protected overhead but was on the deck level, which at the time was fine, but we were back to sea and rolling 35 to 40 degrees, and one of the tins started leaking water into the containers and it started expanding, which broke open another. It was like a chain reaction. When we started the 8 a.m. duty change we were leaving a red, orange and off-white juice behind us. It looked like every shark in the Pacific was following us because of our juices trail, all looking for something to eat. This food filled the passageway and took us several hours to pry, scrap and shovel this out—so slick and sticky, real tough to stand up and work.

While ship was underway at sea, and even nice weather, ship still rolled 25 to 35 degrees. So we had sea rations or make sandwiches, canned meat and fruit. I enjoyed Vienna wieners in cans, spam, pears, peaches. Fruit did not last many days because everyone enjoyed them. You could heat the meat in cans in the second coffee urn, which was hot water. We would drop our can into urn and then fish them out to eat. When at sea we did not have breakfast, lunch or dinner. You were on your own, fix whatever you could.

All watches were 12 hours long. At first when there were two of us on radar, which we operated only at night, I would stand watch every other night. The other nights starboard or port outside watch, or helm watch. It was very tiring and boring. Most of the time when you went to your bunk to sleep you had two or three wide belts you pulled across you and snapped down. These were used so you wouldn't be tossed out of your bunk. Crew all slept in two areas under the galley and officer quarters, a lower and upper bunk. Each had a metal locker. Total height in crew quarters was five feet, seven inches. When bullet holes were made we drove hardwood pegs in them.

Enough of this, we are coming home. Stopped again in Saipan and a storm was coming our way. I thought I was done with typhoons. No such luck, we were in for it with this one. Winds building over 100 m.p.h. Swells were building up to 90 to 100 feet high. All ships must take these head on or you were gone. Ship would come to the top of a swell and start down the screws would come out of the water and ship would shake and down we go; the bow would blow into the bottom all the way back to pilot house and again, shuddering and shaking, the nose starts up, the back goes under water. This goes on hour after hour. This one lasted 14 days. It was not moving across the area with any speed. We were being pushed backwards when we were full ahead with the engines. The radio was being used a lot for us smaller ships, where we could find cover on an island anywhere would help. Also calls like "May Day! May Day!" which means they were in trouble and needed help. This storm sunk seven minesweepers. And at last the storm moved on or played out, we were less than a quarter mile from the rocky shore of Okinawa.

We refueled and headed on to various atolls and islands. Made Hawaii in the middle of the night. Went after mail and boy did we hit the jackpot, as our ship was reported missing and we hadn't received any mail for some time and was held at Pearl Harbor. I swear, most everyone received two mail bags each—Christmas gifts, letters, pictures—it was simply wonderful. In my bag Mom had went to cannery and sealed candy, raisins, dried fruit and popcorn that needed to ship out from Bremerton, Washington.

Anyway, departed about 4 p.m., went on under Golden Gate and weather was stormy and the sea was rough as always. I was sea sick but still on watch. I would say we were 20 to 30 miles out of San Francisco and we hit something pulling one screw and shaft, which left a 12-inch hole in the bottom of the ship and with minutes the other engine was flooded. Quartermaster showed the Skipper how to ring general quarters, which means all personnel report to the upper deck now. Almost all of the deck crew had never been on a ship and most were sea sick and refused to get up. By then water was up to the floor in our quarters. The Boatswain who runs deck crews went to gun locker, got a revolver, loaded it, went down to crew quarters to send a life jacket to each one and told them if they didn't report on deck in foul weather gear and life jacket on in five minutes, he was coming back down and shoot anyone left down there.

We had bilge pumps going full blast, but were not keeping up with water coming in. We had what they call handy billy portable pumps, which helped but still not keeping up with Boatswain and Chief, the extra men bailing water, and wind and rain as well as the tides pushing closer to the rocky shore.

Officers were trying to get help; made the "May Day!" call and several ships replied but were too big and their draft too deep to come this close to shore—it was too shallow. A small tanker running empty came, threw us a line and we sent over a 4-inch rope and they started to tow us. We were moving away from shore, but the rope broke. We spliced it and again we were moving very slow, but moving, and the rope broke again. Again we spliced the break and also sent out a 3-inch line as well, told tanker if he could hold in place as a tug was on its way. By the time the tug arrived we had been running pumps and bailing for almost 30 hours. We were towed back to San Francisco and pulled up to a repair ship. They lifted fantail out of water and welded a steel plate over hole, towed to Hunter Point. New Skipper was removed for running too close to shore. We were to decommission USS YMS-65. She had served us, we had many miles on her; she stayed upright and brought us home. And a lot of young men found it was not all fun and games.

When we had her mothballed and towed away, the crew was reassigned. The Navy was trying to get sailors to volunteer for the atomic bomb test in the Bikini Atoll[14] in the Pacific Ocean. I de-

---

14 Read more about the nuclear testing in the Bikini Atoll here: http://whc.unesco.

clined as I was assigned to help decommission first a large flat bottom craft. These used to land troops and large equipment such as tanks, Jeeps, trucks, etc. The main decks was 40 feet wide and about 600 feet long on each side, 10-foot-wide passageway two decks high with four-high bunks for personnel that would go ashore.

Our jobs were really showing the civilians where items to be mothballed and items to be removed. Also guard duty at night. We were housed and fed on an old ferry. Its rooms and a large center area with 8-high bunks. I helped decommission three of these. When we went and cleaned out the stores, sailors had first choice. There were all types of kitchen ware, knives, forks, spoons, all stainless steel. Cigarettes—oh yes, I bought full case of Philip Morris Cig for $5. There 24 cartons in this case. Sent to Elver Nielson.

I was then sent over to Treasure Island Naval Center, was asked again to go to atomic test and they would pay me $3,000 to go, but what I saw in Japan, I wanted no part of atomic bombs. Then they offered, since I was USNR and they had excess of regular USN personnel, if I would give up my third class and go back to Seaman first class they would discharge me. I did and they sent me by train to Bremerton, Washington for separation. This only took most of one day and gave me a train ticket home.

I should say here that all of the guns I brought home and given to all of my grandsons came from the island that I visited during the war. And with that, enough of the war days.

Home Again

I CAUGHT THE train at Seattle and headed to Nyssa, Oregon. Arrived Nyssa about 5 a.m., checked my seabag and I walked uptown. At a restaurant that was open, as hadn't eaten for some time, ordered coffee and was trying to drink and was really nervous and was spilling more than drinking. My aunt owned the place and she did the cooking and she came out and said she would take me home. And with that the war days are done out in the open and now in our Lord's hands and for everyone to read. I went away a very determined boy and came home still only 19, but a 6-foot, 182-pound man. And home was beyond anything I dreamed about. My mom was as beautiful as ever, the wonderful kisses and hugs. And she smelled like fresh bread. Patty was beautiful and so grown up. Jack had to be one foot taller and the most curly hair, as was a young man.

Betty and Elver looked so good and Gary and Bill had grown and had all kinds of questions about the war and all the things I did. Dad shook my hand and said he was glad that I was home. Dad had told me I would have a tough time adjusting to civilian life. I told the family don't touch me if I'm asleep, just say my name, as I still come awake rather violent and hopefully it will calm down in time. And it took time to make adjustments.

I bought a 1939 Commander Studebaker four-door and told Dad I would try farming. I lasted on the farm until Christmas. Oh yes, I went back to high school half a day, half a year, as I needed two credits to receive a diploma. Patty and a girl named Lorraine Farr were in the same two classes I was in. Lorraine and I started going together and we all graduated in 1947. And we were married in March 1948.

I helped Dad finish the year, told him I wanted to get married and go on to school. He said OK, as he could make out on the farm if I would help with the sugar beet crop. Lorraine (Babe) and I decided to go to Nevada and get married, and by then I had traded my car for a 1937 Chevey. And so off we went early one morning and we were a few miles short of Wilder, Idaho and a rod let go on the engine, poking a hole in the back. I walked to a farm house and called my Dad. He came and towed us home. When pulled into the yard, Elver unloaded us from my car into his 1937 four-door Buick. We made it to Nevada and returned two days later, repaired my Chevey and was helping dad with the beets.

I drove truck and helped with repairs. One day I was welding on some equipment and overhead door was propped up in air about 8 or 9 feet high and it was knocked out and the door, as it swung down, hit me on the back of my head and it knocked me flat and one very large bump on the back. But back to work. A couple days later I was taking a load of beets to town and all at once there was only a half a road. A car was coming and only half of it, the house and cattle, and could only see the right half. Went a mile or so and it went away. This happened several times and one morning we were starting load some beets and Dad was driving a John Deer tractor topping the beets. He needed to go to end of field before he would come over with other tractor with the loader. I had gotten out of truck and trying tell my dad something was wrong with me. I would fall down, get up and go down again. And Dad came over to me, my arms and legs and neck all tried twist completely out of shape. Dad held my head from turning and then man held the arms and a third held my legs. I stopped breathing and become stiff. They loaded me in car, stopped at house, picked up Mom and headed to town. Dad told Mom he thought I was gone. I had turned blue in color on the way to town. They had to cross over railroad tracks as they traveling as fast as they could. The crossing were rough and Mom said I gasped and color started coming back.

Local doctor said to take him to VA Hospital in Boise. Both Babe and Pat worked in town and they came. I was conscious by this time, however when ask my name it took about five minutes to answer. In my mind I answered. They were told not to let me sleep. Pat drove very fast to VA Hospital and this man interviewed only me. He did not ask if I had been hurt, so he sent me to the mental ward. Babe jumped all over the man who took us to this ward. I also said I would not stay there. This man took us to a doctor who took a look at me, sent me in a wheelchair for X-rays and other tests and put me to bed as I had a large blood clot in right leg and smaller ones near heart and head. They put me on heavy doses of blood thinner, told me to stay in bed and when my food [came] it was all soft stuff and a nurse feed it to me. This went on for about a week, when X-rays that clots were gone. I could go home.

    I decided to go to Klamath Falls and go to vocational school at Oregon Tech. I took accounting for refrigeration. Did this for one term, went home. Babe still working in Bank. I worked highway through summer, a temporary job. Went to work in a local filling station for $35 a week, 60 hours first week, 70 hours next week.

    Heard that railroad was reducing work week from 48 hours to 40-hour work week. They needed men. I applied and was accepted. I went to work August 30, 1949 at Nyssa, Oregon as a clerk. Started at night job and after working 10 hours a day, I did not know what to do with all this time off and earning $250 a month. So I took on temporary jobs; bookkeeper for a local drug store, also worked at a grain feed store.

    And lo and behold we had a brand new baby boy born January 20, 1950 named Steven Dell Chard. I worked at Nyssa and Ontario, Oregon; Payette, Weiser, Nampa, Minidoka, and Twin Falls, Idaho. And once again we had another baby boy born July 25, 1953[1] named Lance Matthew Chard. Worked a lot of different jobs and learned a lot from each one.

---

1 Ken misreported the year as 1952.

Vacations with the RR: After one year you earned seven and a half days, and continued through five years. Then went to two weeks for five years. I wanted to tell all of you about our first seven and a half day vacation, of which weekends could be used to make the seven and a half days a little longer. Anyway, we decide to go back to Salina and Lucas, Kansas. So I ordered passes, which allowed us to ride free in chair cars. So off we went. Steven was little over a year old. Went to Lucas first. I had uncles, aunts and cousins at Lucas. Babe had older sister in Salina, borrowed my cousin's 1950 two-door bullet nose Studdebaker and drove to Salina, visited with them a couple of days and started back to Lucas.

We were about 20 miles and it started to rain and then it was beyond rain. It was pouring. Wipers could not keep up. We stopped with all wheels on the pavement and beside us water was washing dirt, etc. away, looked and it had washed dirt down about four feet down and was washing under pavement where we sat. We moved to the center of highway. This downpour lasted 38 minutes and rained 8.5 inches. Radio advised if you were driving you should get to higher ground. We had one river to cross. When we arrived it was starting to run over onto the road. We hurried across the road, was straight for about 15 miles. Road was covered with about one foot of water, so we had to drive slow. We were coming to a 90 degree left turn, water was coming down from hill, shooting up onto and over the highway. To this day I don't know why that car ran and stayed on the road, but we came out the far side car running and we headed down into this little down called Vesper and 90 degrees right there was a hill 80 to 90 feet high and I said where we stay. Highway dipped back down and covered with three feet of water and a Greyhound bus sat in the middle and about this a big red truck coming the other way. They stopped and hooked on to rear of bus, pulling him out and up on hill. This was my two cousins coming after us.

There was another couple from Lucas in a Chevey. They

hooked him up and us behind his car and off we went. Had to go 26 or so miles; in places they were standing on running board to see where the roads was. The car we were in had air vents inside wall where you could open with your feet, as we were going through water up to four and five feet deep and was all the way on windows. Well somehow Babe stepped on hers and water came rushing in and it was cold. She held baby above water while I tried to find out where it was coming from. Found it and we were going over a high place in road, opened both doors and dumped water to the lower part of the seat. Through all of this Steve did not cry or act up. I think he knew we were in trouble. What a great relief it was to reach Lucas. The gals took Babe and Baby to their house, putting them in hot tub or water, fed the baby and he was asleep. Babe, they had mixed her up a hot toddy and a pill and she finally calmed down and also slept.

We took car in shop, removed carpets, seats, drained oil from engine, transmission and differential and we decided to have a drink, or two, three, four and I was cold sober and didn't sleep. Next morning the railroad ran through the outer edge of town and was about four feet above the level of the town. Water was about to run over tracks. My cousin had a boat and we heard cattle bawling and we went looking and we found seven head standing in a 30-foot silo. They had swum to it and crawled in. We roped four of them and swam them to the RR tracks, returned and brought the other three to RR tracks. The little creek that ran south of town about one and a half miles, most of the time six to eight feet wide, was not three miles wide. The electric and telephone poles were completely underwater. The little town of Vesper, Kansas that we went through coming from Salina and we parked on hill above, flood water completely cover all buildings and homes were all underwater. Only the roof of the grain elevator could be seen. The town had moved to the hill and no loss of life was reported.

We phoned Babe's sister in Salina and water came within inches of the front and back door, filled basement with muddy water. They were about two miles from river. When water receded the mud was so hard to shovel. A city truck and crew brought pumps and fire hoses and washed the mud and pumped the basement clean. Furnace and hot water tanks were ruined and they had parked their car on a nearby hill. They only had to replace furnace and the gas unit in water heater. Tough times for a lot of people.

We bought two lots from Babe's folks. I dug a one-half basement and also a septic tank and built a one-story, one-bedroom house. Babe's dad was a very good—no I would say a great—carpenter. He taught me a lot. Many different things. Dad came and helped me put in chimney. I did all of the wiring and plumbing. We heated house with an oil heater.

I was bumped out of Nyssa. Only opening was in Twin Falls, Idaho. Worked in warehouse and we rented a two-room apartment and one trip back from our folks in Nyssa, we were real close to Bliss, Idaho when a valve broke and went down through piston. Car was missing and using a quart of oil every ten miles, leaving a smoke stream behind us. But we made Twin Falls. So each night after work I would work. I had the following tools: pliers, screwdriver, crescent wrench and a lug 3/4-inch socket. I finally got it tore down, removed piston and took it to a Auto Parts and they said it would be $57 for piston gaskets. As we were living on a shoestring budget, I told them to order and I would come up with the money.

Yard was about two feet high of weeds and grass. The owner came by and ask who cut the yard, as this was a four-plex apartment, two downstairs, two upstairs. We were paying $45 a month. He said if we keep the yard up he would reduce rent to $35 a month. He also ask if I could paint and told me he would furnish paint, brushes, ladder, scraper, tape, etc. I did this. This place was made of stone. Each apartment had two wooden frame windows, a front door and a rear door. One window on each side and rear of apartments. All four were alike. Upstairs and rear stairs I did these and cut my rent to $25. I also repaired fence and painted it. And he reduced our rent to $20 a month and he took us to a friend of his that has chickens and he would sell us eggs 10 cents a dozen and fresh fryers for 25 cents a pound. Also ham and bacon and beaf meat for less than half of what the big stores [charged]. As you can see, with these savings I could get the part for the car. Also you could tell we were broke and living payday to payday and by doing these things where we lived we were putting some money away.

Went to pick up parts for car and I paid them and he said that we were having a rough time, so he gave me the 7/16x1/2 sockets and barker bar to fit these sockets and with these parts I repaired car and this was a great day for us. Summer came and was able to bid back to Nyssa at a much higher pay, $300 a month.

Family Life

THINGS WENT WELL for us and the boys. I was asked in 1953 to transfer to the traffic department in Boise, Idaho. I started there at the lowest job and worked my way up, was promoted to traffic agent and traveled all branch lines in the Boise territory. I traveled for several years, was promoted again as Assistant General Agent, putting me as second man in the Idaho territory. I traveled all of the Idaho territory from Utah border, Butte, Montana; McCall, Idaho; Burns, Oregon; Wilder, Idaho; to Huntington, Oregon.

We had bought a house on Grand Street[1] in south Boise. The boys started school there and Steven went to Boise High School and received an appointment to the United States Naval Academy. Lance was involved with band, as he loved music, playing band in grade school as well as when he started high school at Boise High.

Babe was having some health problems. Her father passed away. He was a good man. 1968 Steve was off to the Naval Academy. Lance was starting his sophomore year. I was transferred to Portland, Oregon as assistant freight agent (Freight Rates). Lance and I went to Portland, looking for a place to live. We found an apartment across from high school, so would be close for Lance to go. We finally sold house in Boise and bought a new one in the Rock Creek area. Babe's health not good.

Steve was home for 30 days his sophomore year, and the boys went hunting and target shooting. Lance and I had rebuilt the old VW, removed old body and put a convertible body on the chassis. I was at work and my phone ring and it was Steve—told me Lance had shot himself in the leg. I told him how to get to hospital and I took off from work and met them at hospital. He went to ER and X-ray showed the bullet traveled down upper leg, hitting direct into the large knee bone and lodged under the knee cap. Talked with Doctor and they operated, removing bullet and other particles and put him in a cast. This was about 1 p.m. Had Steve go to store where Babe worked and bring her to hospital. I had to talk with police and

---

1 Now known as Grand Avenue.

tell them how, when, etc. this all happened, as they do this whenever it happens.

We made it home about 4 p.m., just went into house and phone rang and it was my aunt Faye called and told me my mom was in hospital and she would let me know later what they find out. Steve and another boy took VW to the coast and was staying the night down at coast with friends. Eight p.m. my aunt called and said mom had passed away. Like what else could happen. So about 1 a.m. phone rings and Steve said they rolled the VW. The boy wasn't hurt. Steve said his shoulder hurt, but he would drive VW back home next morning. He only got a little ways and called. He could not go any further. So Babe and I went after him. After getting him home, took him to VA hospital and he had a broken shoulder. This put some grey hairs on my head overnight. Kind of like if it rains it pours. Babe, Steve and I drove to Nyssa for mom's funeral, which was on Saturday, and I will say this was one of the toughest weeks I had to face to keep trying to protect my family.

Babe was going downhill. Dad came to visit and she came home for the night from the institution hospital and we had good dinner and we went to bed. About 12 a.m. she was throwing up and so very sick. Dad and I took her back and they checked and said she was having a heart attack and they had called for ambulance moving her to hospital where they could handle heart attacks. They put in a pacemaker to keep her heart in rhythm and after a couple weeks they removed the pacemaker.

The mental problem slowly progressing and no one hated worse than herself. I believe she had inherited this because her mother and two sisters all were treated in institutions. I have a real problem with so called doctors who deal with the mind. She was doing fairly good by taking a pill. He would only allow five pills and I had to call him to get five more. They charged us $50 for each phone call. The store where she worked carried insurance as well as UPRR,[2] my insurance, and they started arguing who was going to pay and this went on several months. I received notice from hospital they were in

---

[2] Union Pacific Railroad.

process of garnishing my wages if not paid by certain date. I knew a Vice President at Amtrak, sent all information and two days later he called and said he had discussed with claims headman and the $15,000 bill would be taken care of. He said the claims people had delayed so they could review charges and advised them to protect our people and if he received another like this heads will roll. I don't know who paid, but all bills were paid and all our future ones taken care of.

Babe wanted to go down to Nyssa for Christmas, so I got a week off and we went down to her mom's first and it was refreshing to hear them talk and her mom was making her a dress and they trying this one and had some coffee and cakes. And about midnight we went to my Dad's house. He just gotten home from hospital party where he worked and he had hard Christmas candy.

Babe was laying on her side talking and kidding about the sack—did it have an orange? And sure enough there was one in bottom. Babe made a gurgling type noise. I went over to her and she was not responding to touch or voice. I put Nitra pills,[3] but nothing changed. My wife May Lorraine Farr Chard was gone. Ambulance came and took her to the morgue. We were married 27 years.

Betty and Elver came and took Dad and I to their place. Next morning called Lance and Steve, made airline ticket for Steve to come from Naval Academy, Lance to drive down. Also phoned my boss at Portland and he told me to take as much time as needed. Somebody picked up Steve in Boise and brought to Nyssa. It was again a tough time. After funeral I worked early to late, of which was my way of work through this heartache. I did some dumb things and was transferred to Omaha, as assistant to the rate department.

---

3 Likely nitrazepam, a hypnotic/sedative drug of the benzodiazepines family often used for the treatment of severe anxiety and insomnia (Mehdi, T. Benzodiazephines Revisited. In British Journal of Medical Practitioners. http://www.bjmp.org/content/benzodiazepines-revisited).

New Beginnings

I rented a house and settled in. I was going to rate meetings and any other rate problems. I was flying to Seattle one week every month, and to San Francisco one week every two months, and to Los Angeles three days every month. Any rate problem in Chicago, Cleveland, Atlanta—it seemed like I was in a plane more than my desk. I was going to Omaha from San Francisco and had a six-hour layover in Denver. I was so tensed and was just sitting and in August 29 would complete my 30 years, so when I was in office I wrote Vice President and ask to retire on that date. He wrote me and confirmed. I was retired from railroad August 29, 1979. Rented a U-Haul trailer and loaded up and 4 a.m. August 30, I was heading to Oregon. Stopped in Nyssa, saw Dad, Betty, Elver, came on, stopped in Hood River and saw Patty and Doyn, then to Portland, rented an apartment, saw Lance and Steve. Lance had a small construction company and I joined him as I always enjoyed carpenter work. Lance started working in sales, so I started a company known as Chard & Co. Worked at many different jobs, generally small repairing or a remodel.

My sister Patty called and said would I go out with a friend she knew and lived here in Portland. I called her and she agreed to have dinner with me. So I went to her apartment and this very attractive lady I meet is Sharon Lee Thompson, who had been married 27 years and now divorced. Come to find out she worked at Albertsons across the street from my apartment. We started dating and we were married March 13, 1981.

We were both working and bid a job in Sherman County. We bought a 30-foot trailer house and went up there and lost money on this job when completed. Took other jobs and never went in the red on any job thereafter. Worked on a ranch one season. Went to work for Steve and we borrowed some money and purchased a business, which went under and lost Sharon's land after son bought it from bank, forced us into bankruptcy. Moved to Redland, Oregon, and lived in basement of Sharon's sister's home. Sharon worked for a sales office. I did odd jobs, anything I could as I had to pay taxes that were never paid when we had the business. I had to make payments for two and a half years to complete the bankruptcy. So this ended that headache and I would advise everybody don't ever get yourself in this kind of mess.

Karen, Sharon's oldest daughter, came up from California and wanted to find a house that we could fix and she [found] a house at 1770 Easy Street in West Linn, Oregon. It needed a lot of work, so I remodeled upstairs, downstairs, roof, windows, siding. Cut down twelve trees in yard, made a deck, front door around corner to the far side of sliding glass door.

Both Peggy's husband Homer and Betty's husband Elver both have passed away. Also Dad. I missed them so very much, I so looked forward to see them when I went to Nyssa. Betty and Peggy had timeshare three-bedroom, unit 53, in McCall, Idaho. And I'm not sure what year they started where we all went to this unit for one week in the fall, which became an annual event for 20 years. We had wonderful food, as Betty, Peggy, Patty, Sharon and Lucy would send food and all of the gals could cook. We played lotto card games, put puzzles together, told stories on each other. This was my highlight of the year. I miss this get together as only Patty and I are left of the five Chard kids that came to Oregon in 1935.

Sharon belonged to a Presbyterian Church, so I joined a church with her and we was married in Presbyterian Church and I have enjoyed the churches. I was slow in letting the Lord in and I have enjoyed him and church very much ever since.

I am going to quote Kane prayer of which I had help with this, but my way of putting it together. This prayer is to my sisters and brother, Betty, Peggy, Jack, Patty and Berl Dean:

Our heavenly father, we thank you for this food, the roof above us and remember that a family is for growing up in, for going away from and for coming back to. It is for loving, concern for helping each oth-

er through happy times and sad. With your blessing, this family will always be together in our hearts and in our memories, giving each of us the strength to live our own lives and to be your own person. Amen.

I love you all so very much. May God bless.

To my sons and their families, I wish only the very best in their young lives. Kenny and Jen and children. Ryan and Molly and their family. Lance and Sari, and Thea. Thea is going to put this in a typed for all to read. I hope she can make sense out of it, misspelled words and all. Bless you, Thea.

Sharon's children Karen, Ron and Jan, I came to love you kids as my very own. To Mark, Andy, Aaron, Brad, Matt and Amanda, you all have made this grandpa a very happy old man. I enjoyed all of you grow to adulthood and now, as in my prayer, you all gone away to grow and raise beautiful families. And you three that are in military, you take extra care as your jobs will and have placed you in hazard areas.

I did not make it to a Vice President with railroad or became a wealthy contractor, but boy have I been blessed with sisters and brother, children, grandchildren and great grandchildren, so the good Lord and I must have done something right. God bless you all. I love you all so very much.

Thank you Mom and Dad for the family of six kids. Bless both of you, Mr. and Mrs. Ewen, and Jessie Chard. I am not sure how to end this, but to all that read this, my greatest hope is that you enjoy this story. I want to say a million thank you's to the person who has put up with all of my many happy times, sad times, sickness, hospital stays. I can't say enough about her—the support, encouragement, and most of all her love. I love you Sharon and again thank you as you are in my prayers each and every day. May God bless.

With that I will say so long. I love all of you.

Dad, Grandpa, Great Grandpa, Ken Chard.

Q&A WITH KEN

AFTER READING THROUGH Ken's memoirs the first time, I sent him a few follow-up questions. While the questions themselves are not intrinsic to the story, the way he approached answering them gives us another insightful slice into Ken and his life.

Q: You say that you and your mother built the family garden together. When I was growing up you always kept a garden. Was this something special that you and your mother shared, a kind of bond between you? Do you have memories of the two of you gardening together?

A: I have always held my mom very high in my life; she and I could talk together. As for garden, we were trying to rise food in those difficult times. Yes, I have many memories of mom and I in the garden. She implanted how to prepare soil, planting seeds, why we kept the weeds out, and how long before items could be used. Lots of hard work and memories that will never leave me.

Q: You talk quite a bit about the times—during the Great Depression and a big drought. How did this affect you growing up?

A: Yes it was tough times for everyone and did it affect us kids, I would say yes. But during this time you did best you could do with what you raised or buy or trade. There were lots of trading in those times. Banks were closed and the little town of Lucas, Kansas made wooden Nickels for trading shopping with. Mom and Dad would trade eggs, cream for groceries. Traded little pigs calves for cattle and hog grains and hay. You could not just drive to store and buy what ever as most likely if you had the money the store would not have it in stock. You could order through the store and would be shipped to them when they received the item. There were a good time before your item was received. I am sure these times did have affect in our later years; the folks had to put up with a lot of stress and worry, and that reflects into us kids as well. We all were more frugal in later years. So yes, it did have affect in our lives, not necessarily bad. We were always a happy family and enjoyed each other and the best we could with what we had.

Q: You tell a story about your mother decapitating bull snakes with a garden hoe. Did you actually witness your mom hoeing the snakes? Do you remember what it was like? The thoughts you had? How does this memory fit into your memory of your mother?

A: Yes, I was there, I saw her kill both snakes. I was pleased because this was two very large snakes that would not be around to steal eggs or baby chicks. Mom was always looking out for us kids health, food-wise, protecting her chicks so to speak. I've always admired this beautiful lady.

Q: You mention that one of your favorite days was butchering day. Why was this one of your favorites?

A: I would say all the hustle and bustle of neighbors coming, men working together doing different jobs, women working making lunch and dinner, also preparing meat, grinding for sausage with all types of seasoning, heating and rendering lard—it was a very exciting day to a young boy.

Q: What's a "squill" on a pig?

A: What is a squill (mispelled) squeal. If you would pinch a girl on the butt she would squeal, which you can't save. Likewise with a pig's squeal it can't be saved either.

About the Author

KEN CHARD PASSED away on December 6, 2012, at the age of 85. This memoir, his first and only work of its kind, was published posthumously in October of 2015.

In his long life, Ken was a homesteader, a cowboy, a seaman, a railroad man, a business owner, a gardener, a golfer and a loving and dedicated husband, father, grandfather, great-grandfather and brother. He is survived by his wife, Sharon, his three sons, two daughters, two daughters-in-law, one son-in-law, nine grandchildren, 14 great-grandchildren and his sister, Patty.

www.ingramcontent.com/pod-product-compliance
Lightning Source LLC
Chambersburg PA
CBHW071356160426
42811CB00112B/2306/J